MW00414316

INSIDE THE JANITORIAL BUSINESS

How to Start from Scratch and Succeed in Professional Cleaning

Second Edition

by Frederick R. Massey

MBM BOOKS, Valley Center, California

INSIDE THE JANITORIAL BUSINESS
How To Start From Scratch And Succeed In Professional Cleaning

by Frederick R. Massey

Published by: MBM BOOKS
                  P.O. Box 1087
                  Valley Center, California 92082 U.S.A.
                  (619) 749-2380

All rights reserved. No part of this book may be reproduced or transmitted in any form or by any means, electronic or mechanical, including photocopying, recording or by any information storage and retrieval system without written permission from the author, except for the inclusion of brief quotations in a review.

Copyright © 1982 and 1989 by Frederick R. Massey
First Edition 1982
Second Printing March, 1983
Third Printing April, 1985
Fourth Printing October, 1986
Fifth Printing April, 1988
Second Edition 1989, Completely Revised

Library of Congress Cataloging in Publication Data

Massey, Frederick R.
        Inside The Janitorial Business:
        How To Start From Scratch And Succeed In Professional Cleaning
        2nd Edition

p. cm.
Includes index
1. Buildings--Cleaning. 2. Self-employed. I. Title
TX958.M27   1989   648'.5'068--dc20   89-2555
ISBN 0-942144-02-3   CIP

Printed in the United States of America

WHAT'S INSIDE

Professional cleaning is one of the last business horizons in North America where you can still start from scratch and achieve your financial goals. Many people know how to do basic cleaning work, but few have discovered the tremendous money making possibilities of the professional cleaning business — a fast growing industry in which anyone can compete.

In these changing economic times just about everyone needs more income. Most people would like to find a way to earn this extra money in a business of their own. *Inside the Janitorial Business* is written with the beginning entrepreneur in mind, the individual who may be low on capital but high on drive, enthusiasm and desire for a better life. If that sounds like you, then you're reading the right book. The information you need to succeed is here in these pages.

You who are already in the business will find this book to be packed with accurate, **inside** information on promoting and expanding your service.

Whether you are looking for a good way to supplement your income or are seeking a whole new business career, you will find this manual invaluable. Get started now and use it as your personal step-by-step roadmap to success in your own professional cleaning business.

ACKNOWLEDGEMENT

My sincere thanks to Kim Fichera, CPA, and to Roger and Judith Frans for their valuable assistance in the production of this book.

This book would be incomplete without expressing my special appreciation to Rosemary Massey, my partner in business and life, for typing, editorial assistance and support in every way. Thanks.

Also by Frederick R. Massey:

The Professional Window Cleaning Manual,
How To Make Money In Your Own Window Cleaning Business

TABLE OF CONTENTS

Chapter 2
STARTING YOUR NEW COMPANY (Continued)

Chapter 3
SELLING YOUR SERVICE... 39

Chapter 3
SELLING YOUR SERVICE (Continued)

Chapter 4
BIDDING AND ESTIMATING..53

Chapter 7
EXPANDING YOUR BUSINESS WITH EMPLOYEES (Continued)

Chapter 8
SUBCONTRACTING 125

Chapter 9
OFFICE CLEANING...130

Chapter 9
OFFICE CLEANING (Continued)

Chapter 10
WINDOW CLEANING..143

Chapter 11
CARPET CLEANING..154

Chapter 12
FLOOR MAINTENANCE (Continued)

Chapter 13
BOOKKEEPING..188

Chapter 14
TAXES...196

Chapter 15
RESOURCES..210

INDEX..216

Chapter 1
THE PROFESSIONAL
CLEANING OPPORTUNITY

There are many ways to create financial success through self-employment, but most new business ventures require a considerable investment of money, specialized training, experience and often a good inside connection.

Professional cleaning is one business that is free of these entry barriers. You may have very little capital, not much cleaning experience and have never owned a business. It doesn't matter. These factors alone cannot stop you if you've got the necessary drive and the following qualities:

1. Determination and enthusiasm
2. Willingness to work
3. Common sense

If you possess these traits, you've got as good a shot as anyone at achieving great success in the professional cleaning business.

There is an almost endless amount of cleaning work to be done all over this country. Think of the countless offices, factories, restaurants, stores and homes. Who cleans all of them? And what about all the new buildings going up every day? Someone must clean them — why not you?

In today's service-oriented world, an ever-increasing number of businesses and homeowners are contracting out their cleaning to professional services. The everyday chore of cleaning has evolved into a specialized business field. No one is in a better position to take advantage of this growing demand than the professional cleaning contractor.

THE KEY TO SUCCESS

The key to success in professional cleaning is to **provide top quality service**. Ask any building owner or manager who contracts out his cleaning. He will tell you how hard it is to locate a good janitorial service. Show him that you can provide the quality cleaning job he needs and you are on your way.

In the beginning, concentrate your promotional efforts on smaller accounts — small offices, banks, stores, doctors' and lawyers' offices, residential work, etc. These accounts are the easiest to bid and clean, and the profit margin is high. With good accounts a one-person business can make $2,500 to $3,500 a month.

You can learn as you go, and work your way up slowly and steadily. Gradually you will gain the experience you need to bid and handle larger and larger accounts. This is the way most of today's successful cleaning contractors started out, including some of the giants in the industry. There is no reason you cannot do the same.

CAN A BEGINNER COMPETE?

You may be thinking, "Sure, but there are already 20,000 people in this business, many of them experts. They have all the accounts locked up and all the connections." Don't kid yourself! This is definitely not a closed industry.

First of all, consider the track record of the competition. What's really going on behind some of your big name competitors with the expensive advertising and professional sales staffs? — crews of underpaid student janitors with impossible work loads — harried supervisors with routes they can't possibly keep up with — quality control that sounds good in a sales pitch, but isn't making it at the working level. In short, very marginal work quality.

This is why so many janitorial companies have a high annual turnover of accounts. They are losing customers almost as fast as they are picking up new ones! These companies are simply too big and inefficient to maintain high quality at the working level, which is all the customer cares about.

Can you compete with these operations? You bet you can! As a small contractor, you can provide superior service and quality control, because you are either doing the work yourself or you are closely supervising it. And, because your overhead is lower than the big companies, you can price your service competitively.

Remember, **a service business is only as good as the people doing the work**. Smooth-talking salesmen don't do the work. You do. So don't underestimate your potential — there will always be room in the professional cleaning business for the person with enthusiasm, dedicated to creating a business based on providing quality cleaning service.

WHAT'S IN THIS BUSINESS FOR YOU?

Here are twelve good reasons to consider launching a business career in professional cleaning:

1. **You are your own boss** — There is no supervisor looking over your shoulder. As an independent cleaning contractor you provide service to many people, but you are never "employed" by them. When you work for yourself you have so much enthusiasm and energy you can do twice the work and still feel great!

2. **Professional cleaning is a dynamic fast-moving business** — You don't have to sit and wait for customers like a storekeeper. You go out and get them.

3. **Work out of your home** — Most maintenance companies start as home-based operations. You can easily operate a good-sized company out of your home.

4. **No inventory** — Because you are providing a service rather than a product, you do not have to carry an expensive, space-consuming inventory. In the beginning your cleaning supplies and equipment can be kept in a garage or storeroom, or even in the trunk of your car.

5. **Small investment required** — The cleaning business is unique in that a beginner can still start with a couple of hundred dollars, or even less, and build a substantial business in a short period of time.

6. **Learn as you go** — You have the opportunity to start with a minimum of experience and learn by doing.

7. **Flexible work hours** — You can run a cleaning service on a part-time basis while continuing a career in another field. Since much of the work must be done in the evenings and on weekends, you can build up your business while keeping your present job. You can also arrange work hours to suit your schedule, one of the really practical benefits of the janitorial contracting business.

8. **Freedom from red tape and regulation** — You do not need a contractor's license to operate. The business is relatively non-unionized, except in some of the larger cities. Paperwork and bookkeeping are simple and straightforward.

9. **Ideal business for a couple** — Running a small janitorial business is perfectly suited to a team of two. Couples who like to work together can find their niche in professional cleaning.

10. **Growth of the market** — The market for cleaning services is virtually unlimited and constantly expanding. Even in hard times, buildings must be cleaned. Cleaning is an ongoing process. The work is never finished — it just keeps coming back!

11. **An open industry** — The janitorial business is not dominated by a few corporate giants with everybody else on the fringe. The small cleaning contractor can hold his own with the big companies. In fact, in many cases he has the advantage.

12. **You can create a valuable asset** — A janitorial business has value in itself. If an employee decides to quit his job or gets fired, he has nothing to show for all the hard work he has put in. But when you have built up a janitorial business **you can sell it for a profit**.

Check the "Business Opportunities" section of the classified ads in your newspaper. Janitorial services of all sizes are going up for sale all the time. But don't buy one! Build your own.

THE PROFESSIONAL CLEANING MARKETPLACE

The whole field of professional cleaning may be broken down into two broad classifications — commercial and residential. Commercial work involves the cleaning of business property, buildings of every size and description — banks, offices, restaurants, stores, industrial plants, etc. Residential work is the cleaning of private dwellings, from studio apartments to mansions.

THE COMMERCIAL CLEANING MARKET

There are many different kinds of commercial accounts. When it comes right down to it, just about every building in sight represents a potential account for the professional cleaning contractor. Here is a brief overview of some businesses that commonly contract out their cleaning.

SMALL OFFICES, insurance offices, lawyers, escrow offices, etc. are probably the easiest of all commercial accounts to maintain and they generally pay very well. Cleaning specifications (tasks) for the average office will usually include trash removal, dusting, vacuuming, restroom care and window cleaning.

Often you can make more money per hour on these smaller accounts than you can on larger ones, but you also have more driving around and set-up time per job. As a result, servicing any one small account may not be highly profitable in itself. However, you can earn excellent money with a group of adjacent or nearby accounts. Once you get one it is easier to get others through customer referral. These small but geographically concentrated accounts are the bread and butter of many a janitorial company.

The trick to offices, as with most cleaning, lies in developing highly efficient work routines. (See Chapter 9)

LARGE OFFICE BUILDINGS — The cleaning specifications for a large office building are usually quite similar to those for a small office. The same tasks are just repeated on a larger scale. It is this standardized aspect of janitorial work that makes it possible to learn on small jobs and gradually work your way up to larger accounts. (See "Cleaning Large Office Buildings", Page 141)

MEDICAL OFFICES — Doctors' offices, dentists' offices and medical buildings of all types are excellent prospects. The work is similar to regular office cleaning, but it requires a little more time and care. People in the medical profession are often very particular about the cleaning of their facilities, for good reason. Medical offices generally pay a little better than regular offices of the same size.

BANKS AND SAVINGS & LOANS often hire one contractor to handle the maintenance for a number of their branches. These accounts pay well. In fact, you can make more money cleaning several banks in the evening or morning hours than the average person makes on a full-time job!

The work is easy and straightforward. Since banks generally consist of one large lobby area and several smaller offices, they can be cleaned faster than office buildings of the same size. The open carpeted or tiled lobby areas can be vacuumed or dust mopped at top speed.

Banks close early in the day, so you can start your cleaning routine in the early evening. And they don't open until late in the morning (usually 9 a.m. or so), allowing you to clean in the early morning hours. Banks close for all the holidays and stay closed on weekends, making for an easy work schedule.

RESTAURANTS AND BARS — Most restaurants and bars have difficulty finding and keeping cleaning services. There are two main reasons — it is hard, greasy work and the hours are rough.

Cleaning restaurants is hard because the grease generated from the cooking spreads in the air and settles on everything, causing surfaces to attract dirt and vacuums to clog up. Also the lighting in the dining room areas is usually poor, making it hard to clean efficiently.

Most restaurants are open seven days a week and must be cleaned each night after 11 or 12 p.m. and before 6 or 7 a.m. Large cleaning companies often avoid restaurants and bars because they have found they cannot find reliable, sober employees who will work these hours and do an acceptable job. Even so, some contractors do specialize in restaurant cleaning and have found it to be a lucrative field. By being well-organized and using the right cleaning products and equipment, they are able to clean restaurants rapidly and efficiently.

Restaurant maintenance offers the beginner an opportunity to build up a considerable volume of business in a short period of time. It can support you while you develop other accounts. When you get better established you can always phase the restaurants out, or subcontract them. Who knows? — you may find you like restaurant maintenance work.

The cleaning responsibilities that many restaurants hire out are the kitchen and dining room floors, restrooms, trash removal and windows. They have their own people do the rest of the detail cleaning.

RETAIL STORES — Many retail businesses contract out their cleaning. Gift shops, hair salons, pharmacies, convenience stores, etc. are all good prospects. What most retail stores are looking for is top quality floor care and window cleaning. (Dusting and general cleaning are usually performed by the employees in their spare moments.) For example, a small gift shop might want you to come in once a week to wax or buff the tile floor, and once a month to clean the windows.

Large retail stores such as supermarkets or department stores are another matter altogether. Floor maintenance on a large scale is a highly technical field. It requires considerable experience and a substantial investment in specialized equipment (such as automatic scrubbers and high speed burnishers). If you are new to the business, you will have to get a good deal of experience under your belt before you tackle the big chain stores.

PROPERTY MANAGEMENT COMPANIES — Many owners of commercial buildings are turning over their management chores to professional property management firms. For a fee, these companies line up the services required to maintain the property, everything from air conditioning to window cleaning. They are constantly looking for reliable services, and if they like your company they are in a position to send you a lot more work. Establishing a good working relationship with one or more property management companies can cause your business to skyrocket.

Property managers operate on a tight budget and this makes them price conscious. But price is not their only consideration. They must also look for quality and reliability in the services they choose, because their reputation depends on securing good services for the buildings they manage.

Property managers are usually more sophisticated in the purchase of services than the average business owner. They deal with service contracts, bids and proposals on a daily basis, and they usually know what the going rate is. To win their business you will need to sharpen your pencil, price your service right and package your bid in a professional-looking proposal. (See Chapter 5)

INDUSTRIAL ACCOUNTS — The beginner need not be overwhelmed by the size of a factory or plant. In many cases the cleaning specifications will be quite manageable. They may only include the executive offices, restrooms and lobby areas — perhaps no more than two or three man hours a day. Or possibly a 10,000 square foot workroom floor is to be swept daily. With a large dust mop you can do the whole floor in an hour. If there are a lot of obstacles, you can use a smaller mop and still get the work done in a reasonable time.

Cleaning the offices and restrooms in a manufacturing plant takes longer than cleaning professional offices. There is always more dust, dirt and clutter in a plant.

GOVERNMENT BUILDINGS — Local, state and federal government agencies often contract out their cleaning. Sometimes smaller government offices such as libraries, municipal buildings, post offices, etc. are good prospects for the beginning cleaning contractor. As you would expect, the process of hiring in these accounts involves piles of paperwork and the bidding is highly competitive.

A beginner is inclined to think, "If I could only get a big, juicy government contract, I'd be all set." The problem is that many government agencies are obligated to accept the lowest bidder who meets their minimum requirements. Consequently, the winning bids on these accounts are usually too low to be profitable and the quality of the work provided is often poor. If you are trying to build a dynamic, quality-oriented business you don't need low pay, low quality contracts.

CONDOMINIUM AND RESIDENTIAL DEVELOPMENTS often contract out the cleaning of their common areas. This might include clubhouses, community recreation centers, pool areas, tennis courts, etc.

In dealing with these accounts you will usually be going through a homeowners' association, a property management firm or some type of committee. If you provide residential services, these "clubhouse" accounts are a gold mine of opportunities to do business with the homeowners themselves.

REAL ESTATE FIRMS — Today's real estate companies are getting more and more involved in leasing business space, managing rentals, etc. They are always in need of cleaning services. If the realtors know you do good work, they will call you and refer you to their clients.

Working for real estate developers is also an open door to all the work available from the construction industry, such as new construction clean-up and cleaning model homes.

WORKING FOR OTHER CLEANING CONTRACTORS — There is a good deal of subcontracting going on in professional cleaning today. Some cleaning companies work exclusively with subcontractors (independent contractors) rather than employees. They find it easier and more profitable to hire subcontractors rather than hire, train and supervise their own employees.

These companies are always on the lookout for small, owner-operated cleaning companies to handle their accounts. Subcontract work won't usually pay as well as your own accounts (because of the middleman), but it is one way for a beginner to get started and gain some valuable experience.

Sometimes when an out-of-town contractor picks up a chain of banks, restaurants or stores (or any other job out of his area), he will find a local contractor to handle the work on a subcontract basis.

Keep an eye on the classified ads, "Help Wanted" listings, for these types of subcontracting opportunities. (For more on subcontracting, see Chapter 8.)

THE RESIDENTIAL CLEANING MARKET

The residential cleaning market has expanded dramatically in recent years and is still growing at a rapid rate. This is largely due to the increasing number of women working outside the home. Two income families have little time or energy left over to take care of all the cleaning that has to be done. They also have more money to spend on all types of services. Residential work can be broken down into one-time jobs and regularly scheduled cleaning (maid service).

ONE-TIME JOBS — One-time work in homes involves such tasks as floor stripping and waxing, and the cleaning of windows, carpets, drapes, blinds, upholstery, etc. (as opposed to general housecleaning).

Many firms that concentrate on commercial work also take on specialized residential jobs. There is good money in providing these services. For instance, a maintenance company may charge $75 to strip and wax a kitchen and dining room floor, a job that takes one and a half hours. The customer is willing to pay a decent price because the contractor has the equipment and the know-how to get the job done right.

Because of the earnings potential, there are many cleaning companies that specialize exclusively in just one or two aspects of residential cleaning — floor care, blind cleaning, window cleaning, drapery cleaning, etc.

Another bonus of residential work is that small jobs well done can be stepping stones to lucrative commercial accounts. Many of your homeowner customers are the prosperous owners or managers of businesses that require maintenance services. If they like your work they may want you to give them a bid on their business cleaning needs also.

HOUSECLEANING OR MAID SERVICES — Regularly scheduled house-cleaning is the residential equivalent of commercial contract cleaning. Housecleaning companies range in size from one person businesses that clean just a few homes to large national firms employing hundreds of workers with annual income in the millions. Recently, seeing the profit potential, many large commercial cleaning contractors have branched out into the residential market. And still the surface has barely been scratched.

Many large housecleaning firms started out literally from scratch. Not surprisingly, a number of these successful housecleaning contractors are women. These women entrepreneurs saw their opportunity and they have taken advantage of it. The days of the old, tired scrubmaid are gone. House-cleaning in this day and age is big business.

Chapter 2
STARTING YOUR NEW COMPANY

Starting a service business is easier than most people realize. The vague fear that there is some complicated procedure involved scares many capable people away from self-employment.

LEGAL STRUCTURE

Once you have made the decision to embark on a new business venture, your first step is to determine what legal form your business will take — sole proprietorship, partnership, corporation or S corporation.

SOLE PROPRIETORSHIP — Most new service businesses are operating as sole proprietorships — one individual, couple or family runs the business. This is the least expensive and simplest form of ownership. All you do is start. A sole proprietorship is subject to the least amount of government regulation. After the business has grown it can be incorporated if the owner desires, but many large, successful services remain as sole proprietorships.

As a sole proprietor, you run the business, make the decisions and are directly entitled to the profits of your business. You are also personally liable for any debts or legal judgments against you. The sole proprietorship does not pay income taxes as a business. You include your business profit (or loss) on your personal tax return.

PARTNERSHIP — In a partnership the business is owned by yourself and one or more other people. The partnership itself pays no tax. Each partner reports their share of the profit on their own personal tax return.

Partnerships are often established to spread the workload between two or more people. They are most beneficial when each individual has something special to contribute to the relationship. For instance, new partners may contribute capital, managerial or sales abilities or other skills. One partner can take time off while the other runs the business. Partners can also lend each other moral support when times are rough.

Although partnerships offer obvious advantages, there can also be serious drawbacks. Like marriage, a partnership is a complex relationship that

22

requires a lot of give and take to be successful. Running a business requires constant decisions — what to do, how to do it, how much to charge, how to treat the employees and so on. When these decisions are shared, disagreements are inevitable. This can quickly lead to bad feelings, arguments and frustration and the rapid demise of the business. Partnership horror stories abound!

Many people are not aware that each partner bears responsibility for the whole business. This means that if there is a judgment against the business and your partner cannot pay his rightful portion, you can be held responsible for the whole debt. It may not always be fair, but that's the way it is.

Going into partnership involves a legal transfer of a portion of your business to another person. If you are thinking of going into a partnership be sure you know your prospective partner well — **very well**. Take some time in the beginning, before signing anything, to discuss your business plans and goals in depth. Make sure you see eye-to-eye on how the business will be run. If you have basic disagreements at this stage, better not go into partnership — you'll almost certainly regret it later.

Although not required by law, it is advisable for new partners to outline all the terms and conditions of their business relationship in a **written** partnership agreement.

CORPORATION — A corporation is a separate legal entity, apart from its owners, which is set up according to state and federal regulations. Corporations do not have to be "big". In most states one person can form a corporation. The main advantage of incorporation is that, as a rule, you are not personally liable for the debts of the corporation. That means if there is a lawsuit or you can't pay your debts, the lawyers and creditors can only press their claims against the business and its assets. They can't come after your house or your car.

Corporations are taxed differently than sole proprietors and partnerships. Corporate profits are taxed twice, first as income to the corporation and then again when distributed to the shareholders (owners). Corporations are also subject to a good deal of ongoing government regulation, which creates additional paperwork and expense. On the other hand, a corporation can hire its owners as employees, pay them a wage and offer fringe benefits such as health insurance. These are all tax-deductible business expenses to the corporation.

Setting up a corporation is relatively expensive compared to the other business forms. By the time you've paid all the fees and the lawyers, you can spend anywhere from a few hundred dollars to three thousand dollars or more.

S CORPORATION — The S corporation (formerly known as Subchapter S corporation) is a special form of corporation with certain tax advantages. With an S corporation you get basically the same limited liability protection of a regular corporation without the double taxation. There is no corporate income tax on an S corporation. Instead, the income and expenses of the corporation are divided among its shareholders (owners), who then report them on their own income tax returns. To qualify for S corporation status, a corporation must have no more than 35 stockholders, issue only one class of stock and meet several other requirements. For full details see IRS Publication #589, "Tax Information on S Corporations".

If you are uncertain about what business form to choose, consult an attorney.

NAMING YOUR BUSINESS

It's your business and you can call it whatever you like, as long as no one else is already using the name. You can name your company after yourself, but this can have its disadvantages. Your new company won't appear to be as big and well-established. Also remember that if you someday decide to sell your business you will be selling your business name as well. Fred's Janitorial Service is not quite the same without Fred.

Now and then you see a maintenance company with a wild, exotic name. As a matter of practicality, however, it is usually best to choose a name that clearly indicates the service you are offering. If you plan to specialize in a particular area give your company a name that indicates this, but if you aren't sure, don't limit yourself by using a specialized name.

If you don't have anything particular in mind, you can give your company a name that starts with "A". Then your name will be one of the first in the Yellow Pages.

To avoid legal problems you must make sure your new name isn't already being used by someone else. If you live in an area that requires filing of a fictitious business name, the county clerk's office should have a complete listing of all fictitious names currently being used in your county.

However, corporations have the right to use their corporate name anywhere in the state, even if they haven't filed a fictitious name statement in your county. You should contact the Secretary of State for your state to find out if the name you want to use is already being used by a corporation. (Look in the phone book under State Government Offices — "Secretary of State".)

You should also check the Federal Trademark Register available at many libraries to find out about names that are being used by national companies.

FICTITIOUS BUSINESS NAME

In most areas if you choose to call your company by any name other than your own, you will be required to file a fictitious business name (also called DBA, "doing business as"). Filing a fictitious business name keeps other people from using the same name in your area. Banks will often require a copy of your fictitious name statement before opening a business account for you.

Filing a fictitious name is a simple, inexpensive procedure. First, go to the county clerk's office and check the lists to be sure the name you want is not already in use. Next, fill out a form and pay a small fee — $10 is common. Then you must have the name published in a newspaper "of general circulation" in your area. In many areas there are small newspapers that specialize in running legal ads. These papers usually charge less than the regular newspapers. You will usually need to renew your fictitious name periodically — every five years is common.

The easiest way to find out about fictitious name requirements in your area is to look in the phone book under "County Clerk" or "Fictitious Names". Just give them a call and they will tell you exactly what to do.

BUSINESS LICENSES

Most cities and some states require you to have a business license. These licensing agencies don't require any proof of your qualifications to run a business. The license requirement is simply a way for local governments to collect tax revenues and keep track of you. Fortunately, the fee for a business license is nominal in most places. If your business is located in an unincorporated town or county area you may not need a business license at all.

To find out about business license requirements in your area, ask a local business person or look in the phone book under "City Clerk", "Business Licenses" or "County Clerk". Any of these agencies should be able to give you the information or steer you in the right direction. They can also fill you in on any other local regulations you must abide by.

YOUR BUSINESS LOCATION

Many service businesses are run out of the owner's home. This is a convenient arrangement which keeps your overhead and start-up costs to a minimum. You can always move to a larger location later, when you have expanded sufficiently to warrant it.

If you have a spare room that you can set aside as an office, you can take a number of income tax deductions. However the IRS is very particular about home office deductions. You must use your office exclusively for business purposes to qualify for a tax write-off. (See page 200, "Business Use Of Your Home")

Some people are afraid that using their home address will make them appear small or unprofessional. There is also the possibility of customers coming around, although they rarely have cause to visit a janitorial business personally. If you are concerned, simply take out a post office box and use that as your business address. Then no one knows where your office is. Many large companies in all areas of business are using P.O. boxes these days. If you plan to apply for a P.O. box, do so right away as there is often a waiting period.

Sometimes local codes prohibit operating a business in a residential area. Even so you'll find some of your neighbors have offices in their homes. Since you will be working elsewhere and there won't be any customers coming and going, you are not really "operating a business" at your home. And no one is likely to complain.

BUSINESS TELEPHONE

Ideally, it is best to have a separate telephone number for your business. Many services are able to manage using only one phone, but there are problems with this. While a family member is talking to friends, potential customers are getting a busy signal. There is also the tendency to answer with "hello" rather than with your business name. If you have children in your home they will be answering the phone and so on.

Having a separate business telephone makes it easier to calculate your taxes. Instead of trying to determine what percentage of your home phone bill is deductible for business, you simply write off the whole amount of the business phone bill.

As with your P.O. box, be sure to apply for your business phone right away. There may be a waiting period and you won't be able to order business checks or have stationery printed until you've got your number.

NOTE: The post office or telephone company may tell you what your box number or telephone number will tentatively be at the time you apply. Be careful! Don't have your stationery or checks printed with these numbers until you've actually got the box or have had the phone line installed. Occasionally, for "reasons beyond their control", the number has to be changed. Then you've got a whole stack of stationery with the wrong address or telephone number on it — expensive scratch paper.

MANNING THE TELEPHONE

Many of your prospective customers will initially contact you over the phone. And your main point of contact with existing customers will be the telephone. That means someone or something must man the phone at all times.

If you are married and your spouse is home most of the time, that's ideal for a small business. If you are single or your spouse works, then you've got three basic alternatives:

1. **Hire a full-time secretary** — an ideal solution, but this is an expensive luxury that most new cleaning services can't afford.

2. **Hire an answering service** — unfortunately, it is about as hard to find a good answering service as it is to find a good janitorial service. If someone you know has had success with one, you could give them a try.

3. **Use a telephone answering machine** — the least expensive option and probably the best way to go. Your success with an answering machine will depend to a great extent on how prompt you are in returning calls. Be sure the machine you purchase allows your callers to talk as long as they want, without cutting them off after a certain number of seconds. You don't want to miss important information, like the last three digits of a prospective customer's telephone number!

BUSINESS BANK ACCOUNT

A business checking account is essential. You should channel **all** of your business income and expenses through this account. It serves to keep your personal finances separate from your business dealings, and the cancelled checks serve as receipts to help document your business expenses. Your checkbook will be the basis of your whole bookkeeping system.

When you go to your bank the new accounts clerk will show you a variety of business checking account systems with varying prices. You don't need anything fancy. Remember, your customers don't see your checks.

Most banks now offer interest-bearing checking accounts for sole proprietors. Be sure to ask about them.

EQUIPMENT AND SUPPLIES

The initial outlay of money for equipment and supplies in the janitorial business is small compared to what it takes to get started in most other businesses. However, this small investment must be well spent to get the essential cleaning tools and supplies you need.

Good quality is always a good investment. Dependable equipment and top quality supplies will save your nerves as well as your money. If you buy inferior quality you will have increased breakdowns, headaches and maintenance costs, and the equipment will have to be replaced much sooner.

Labor costs are always a cleaning contractor's biggest expense. As much as 90% of your operating expense will be labor. Any inferior equipment that slows your workers down is going to cost you a bundle over the long run. There is always a time factor in contract cleaning. Equipment failure can wreak havoc when you are operating on a tight schedule. You need to take all these factors into account before you put your money down.

WHERE TO BUY YOUR EQUIPMENT AND SUPPLIES

Generally it's best to buy your supplies and equipment from a **local** janitorial supplier. You need someone who can give you on-the-spot advice and recommend products for your specific needs, as well as provide service for your equipment. Sometimes a local supplier can even give you a tip on where to pick up a new account.

If you are just starting a new business you should take the time to visit all the local janitorial suppliers. Walk around their stores, talk with the owners or salespeople and compare prices. Look for knowledgeable salespeople who will take the time to talk with you. You can learn a lot this way. Most janitorial supply stores are retail outlets that sell to the general public and institutions, as well as to contractors. They will often give you a discount for being in the business.

There are also several national suppliers that sell cleaning equipment and supplies directly through the mail. You can find some excellent buys from these large volume distributors. It will pay you to get their catalogs and compare prices. (See the Resources chapter.)

If you shop carefully you can get started in basic office cleaning with a total equipment cost of less than $250 — even less if you can find good used equipment.

LOCATING GOOD USED EQUIPMENT

Contractors who are just getting started and are operating on a limited budget should look into buying as much good used equipment as possible. Quality commercial cleaning equipment is built to last. When established companies purchase new equipment they often sell off their old machines. You can find these used machines by watching the classified ads ("Miscellaneous for sale", "Business equipment for sale") and by going around to the local janitorial supply stores. They often have used machines. Other likely sources of used equipment include vacuum repair shops, swap meets and appliance repair stores. The ideal situation is to find someone who is going out of business and buy everything they've got.

Many of your tools can be put to use in a variety of ways to save buying specialized items. As you build your business and encounter new cleaning situations, you will gradually acquire a full range of janitorial specialty tools and equipment. The exact equipment and supplies you will need for specific types of cleaning are discussed in detail in Chapters 9 through 12.

VEHICLE

In the beginning you can usually operate with your own car, especially if you have a truck, van, station wagon or hatchback coupe. By using a magnetic sign you can transfer your advertising from one vehicle to the other. You don't necessarily want to paint up the family car!

Minipickups (with a shell) and small vans are ideal because of their excellent gas mileage. You will have plenty of room and be able to get to all your tools easily. If you install a roof rack you can carry several ladders on the roof.

Whatever kind of vehicle you use, it needs to be reliable. Much of this work is done after hours, so you've got to be able to depend on your wheels. You must also be able to lock your auto — some people do steal janitorial equipment. Be sure to mark your larger equipment with some form of identification.

SETTING UP YOUR OFFICE

Fortunately you don't need a lot of expensive oak furniture and computer hardware to get started in the cleaning business. All you need are a few basic pieces of office equipment to use in preparing your paperwork and some basic office supplies.

OFFICE EQUIPMENT

Typewriter — A typewriter is helpful for the preparation of professional-looking letters, advertising material and proposals. This doesn't mean you need to pay $1,000 for a new IBM Wheelwriter. In the beginning any good, used typewriter will do. They are available everywhere at reasonable prices. You can also rent a good machine for a modest monthly fee, anywhere from $20 to $50. If you don't type, find a nearby typist or secretarial service to do it for you.

Desktop calculator — A desktop calculator with a tape for adding figures is essential for your bookkeeping. It will also save you a lot of time when you are preparing estimates and bids.

OFFICE SUPPLIES

Letterhead stationery and envelopes
Plain white paper (for your file copies)
Carbon paper
Billing statements
3x5 or 4x6 cards
    (for customer records and reminder cards)
File boxes (for cards)
Manilla file folders
    (one for each regular commercial account)
Stapler
Phone message pads
Receipt book
    (for jobs that pay on the spot. Keep in vehicle.)
Petty cash box
Clipboard
Rubber stamps
    (one with your company name and address, the other for bank deposits)
Dictionary
Street atlas (book of maps of your area)
Bulletin board
Large desk calendar
    (to save you from forgetting or doubling up on appointments. Keep by the phone.)
A reliable alarm clock
An answering machine

MONEY MATTERS

Traditionally, obtaining funds from commercial lenders for new service businesses has been no easy task. In today's economy it is next to impossible, so don't plan on getting a start-up loan from your friendly local banker.

What about the Small Business Administration? Don't count on it. Even if you are able to wade through the red tape you may be old and gray before you get your loan, if you get it at all.

If you absolutely must borrow, your relatives and friends are probably your best bet. As we all know, these situations can get very messy and spoil relationships, so be careful.

If at all humanly possible, find a way to get started without borrowing. Professional cleaning is without a doubt one of the easiest businesses to begin, from the standpoint of required start-up capital. If you start small you can get off the ground with surprisingly little money. This is one of the real advantages of going into this field in the first place. So don't get over a financial barrel right from the start. Find another way. It is much better to start out on a part-time basis and let your present job pay the bills while your business grows.

If you are unemployed you could consider going to work for another maintenance company while starting your own on the side. (You don't have to publicize it!) You can acquire valuable experience and pick up the tricks of the trade, while getting a start at the same time. There is always a way.

BUSINESS INSURANCE

Find a good insurance agent, one who is familiar with writing liability and property damage policies for service businesses. Ask around, talk with other local business owners and get references. Look for a knowledgeable agent who will take an interest in your business and spend the time necessary to determine your insurance needs.

The most important type of insurance for your business is **liability insurance**. Liability coverage protects you against financial disaster if you are sued for injuring someone or damaging their property in the course of your business. "Bodily injury" and "property damage" are the two essential coverages.

Your liability policy should also include coverage for "completed operations". This insurance protects you against claims arising from the work you've done **after** you have left the job site. (The classic example is someone falling down and hurting themselves on a newly-waxed floor.)

If you have employees, your liability policy should include "non-owned" auto liability insurance. This protects you if one of your employees has an accident while driving his own car, in the course of working for you. If you work with independent contractors you should also carry "owners' and contractors' protective liability", which protects you against acts by your subcontractors. This is an inexpensive coverage which could save you a lot of grief someday.

Your liability rates are based on your annual payroll. The more employees you have the greater your exposure and the more you pay. If you have no employees you will still be charged a minimum amount based on "owner's payroll". Liability rates are often quoted as a certain dollar amount per $100 of payroll. For example, if your rate is $2.94 per $100 and you have $21,000 of payroll, your annual premium would be $617.40 per year ($21,000 ÷ $100 x $2.94).

When you are first starting, your initial premium will be based on an estimate of your expected payroll for the year. Then at the end of the year the insurance company will audit your operations to see what your actual payroll has been. This audit is not like the infamous IRS audit! Usually the insurance company just mails you a form to fill out indicating how much payroll expense you had for the period being audited. If your actual payroll was lower than estimated you will get a refund or a credit. But if you have had more payroll than you estimated they will send you a supplemental bill, which can be quite a shock if you are not expecting it.

Insurance is the biggest start-up expense for most new contractors. When you are just starting out it can be very difficult to raise or budget the money for an insurance policy. The fact is, many businesses simply do without insurance in the beginning. They have decided to take the risk rather than spend the money. But one lawsuit, legitimate or not, can wipe you out financially. Even if you win the lawyer fees alone can bankrupt you.

Businesses in this "sue-happy" day and age need the protection afforded by insurance. If you have been operating without it, make it a top priority to start setting aside money and get yourself covered.

Insurance rates and coverages provided vary from one company to the next, so it will pay you to shop around and get several quotes. You might want to check with independent agents who work with a number of insurance companies. They can check with their sources and give you some comparative prices and plans.

One way to reduce rates is to go with high deductibles and pay for any small damages out of pocket. This makes good sense because what you really are buying insurance for is to protect against the catastrophic losses. You don't want to hassle your customers and the insurer with small claims anyway.

You should also look for an insurance plan that will allow you to pay the premiums in installments. This is important because you don't want to put out any more cash up front than you have to. The cost of insurance is much easier to bear if you are able to spread the expense out and pay your premiums out of the profits as you go along.

THERE IS MORE TO INSURANCE THAN PROTECTION

In the janitorial business there is a good deal more to insurance than financial protection. It could easily be the difference between getting an important bid or not. Many potential customers want to be assured that you carry insurance. Including this information on your business cards, advertising and promotional material helps greatly to establish your credibility.

Once you are insured you can request a "Certificate of Insurance" from your insurance company. This is a standard form which shows your company name and the types and amounts of your coverage. This certificate provides proof of your insurance to your customers and you can also include it with your bids and proposals to help win jobs.

If you plan to become an employer you will be required by your state to carry Workmen's Compensation insurance. (See page 124) Workmen's Compensation insurance is usually administered by a state board, but your insurance agent should be able to obtain this coverage for you, or put you in touch with the agency that can.

BONDING

The two basic types of bonds used in the janitorial industry are fidelity bonds and surety bonds.

FIDELITY BONDS — A fidelity bond protects you and your customers against theft by your employees. It is a good idea to get this type of bonding even if you do not plan to employ anyone. Just the fact that you are "insured and bonded" makes customers feel more comfortable about having you working in their buildings.

There are three types of fidelity bonds: individual, schedule and blanket. Individual bonds name a specific person; schedule bonds list all the names or positions to be covered; and blanket bonds cover all employees but do not identify them by name or position. The blanket bond, which covers all workers including those hired after the bond goes into effect, is the bond most commonly used by janitorial services.

Many of your customers don't really know what kind of protection a fidelity bond provides them, if any! They just feel that you should be bonded — it sounds safe.

The fact is, in order for the bonding company to be required to reimburse the customer it must be **proven** that you or your employees have stolen from them. Not only must a theft occur, but the responsible employee must be caught, tried and convicted. Just because something disappears mysteriously does not obligate the bonding company to pay up on a fidelity bond.

Still, from the standpoint of marketing your service and establishing credibility with potential customers, being "bonded" helps. Fidelity bonds aren't expensive. You can obtain one through your insurance agent.

SURETY BONDS — Some very large accounts and government contracts may require you to obtain a **surety bond** as a condition of awarding you a bid. Surety bonds (sometimes called performance bonds) guarantee your customer that you will complete and fulfill the terms of your contract. Basically if you can't complete the job, the company that issues the performance bond (the surety company) must do so. If the surety company must step in and arrange to finish the job, they have the right to collect from you any costs they incur. As you can imagine, this type of bonding is expensive and hard to get.

The surety company will take a close look at your company's financial statements and experience. And you will have to put up collateral before they will issue you a bond. Fortunately, unless you are bidding on very large commercial or government contracts, you will seldom be required to obtain a performance bond for janitorial work.

STATIONERY AND BUSINESS CARDS

Stationery and business cards are an important part of your promotional effort. When you've got your address, phone number and business name finalized you should arrange right away to have cards and stationery printed up. Make a few phone calls to local printers to compare prices, as they do vary substantially.

Don't spend time now trying to develop a perfect graphic design or logo. Just go ahead with a simple, inexpensive format. Have a small number of cards and letterhead printed, perhaps 500. This will get you started. While you're using up this first order of stationery and cards you will have time to develop a logo and a design that you will be really pleased with.

PROFESSIONAL HELP

There are times when the services of a good lawyer or accountant are invaluable. However, you do not need to seek professional help every time a routine question comes up. Often with a little initiative you can get the answers you need elsewhere, for free.

A great deal of information can be found in the public library. Also the Small Business Administration and SCORE (Senior Corps Of Retired Executives) can be of service. SCORE is an organization of retired executives who volunteer their services to help beginners get started in business. Look them up in the phone book under the U.S. Government listing for the Small Business Administration.

People in this business are, by and large, friendly and helpful. By asking questions you can learn a lot in a hurry. You may also find that a 20 cent phone call to the appropriate government agency will provide the answers to your questions.

The everyday administrative paperwork involved in filing for a fictitious name, applying for a business license or an employer's I.D. number should not require professional assistance. On the other hand, if you are considering going into a limited partnership or buying an existing business, it could be disastrous not to obtain professional help.

Use your common sense and retain a lawyer or accountant only in those situations that warrant it.

START-UP ALTERNATIVES

Besides starting your own business from scratch, there are three other ways of getting started in the professional cleaning business:
1. Buy an existing business.
2. Purchase janitorial accounts.
3. Invest in a franchise.

BUYING AN EXISTING JANITORIAL BUSINESS

Some people prefer to buy an existing business rather than start their own from scratch. When you buy a cleaning business you usually won't get much in the way of tangible assets — cleaning equipment, supplies, inventory, etc. The two most important things you get are customer accounts and goodwill.

Customer accounts — This is where the real value in any janitorial service lies. **This is the income.** When you buy a janitorial contracting business you must be sure you are getting good customers with solid contracts. Under no circumstances should you purchase a cleaning business without personally inspecting the accounts and speaking with the customers.

You should have a clear understanding of your responsibilities and the assurance of the customers that you will in fact be retained as the new cleaning contractor. While it is true that many janitorial contracts are set up to run a year or longer, they also usually include a 30-day written notice (cancellation clause), allowing either party to terminate the agreement if it becomes unsatisfactory. You don't want to pay good money for weak accounts that are about to be cancelled!

To protect yourself, you should insist on a written guarantee, which provides for a prorated refund or reduction in payments in the event you lose accounts (through no fault of your own) within a certain period of time. The seller should also be required to provide you with proper orientation and training on each account.

Goodwill — This is the company's name and reputation. It is the accumulative effect of jobs well done, word of mouth and advertising over the years. It includes all of a company's contacts with the public, suppliers and other businesses. Goodwill is an "intangible" asset. You can't hold it in your hand, but it is extremely valuable. Goodwill has much to do with a company's ability to grow and acquire new business. If you are able to purchase a company with goodwill and a strong reputation, you are way ahead.

Unfortunately, what many business sellers have to offer could best be described as "badwill"! The service has been poor, the clients are complaining and cancelling and the owner is burned out. That's why he is selling his business in the first place. Buying a business such as this is not an opportunity — it is a nightmare. You need to investigate the business thoroughly to make sure you are not buying a lemon.

When you purchase a business you should always have a "covenant not to compete" agreement written into the sales contract. This prevents the former owner from turning right around and starting a new cleaning business in competition with you.

Most businesses for sale are priced way too high (like autos and homes), with the idea of allowing the seller to negotiate down to the price he really wants. Terms of payment vary from one situation to the next — generally the more favorable the terms, the higher the price. But everything is negotiable.

36

In some rare cases a seller may hold out for full payment before turning over the business. However, most people who are interested in starting a maintenance business do not have access to that kind of money. Consequently most business purchase agreements involve a down payment with the balance being financed over a number of months or years. In this way the new owner is able to pay for the business out of the income it generates.

PURCHASING JANITORIAL ACCOUNTS

One way for a beginner to get a foothold in the business is to purchase janitorial accounts from another contractor. In this case you are not buying a business, just cleaning contracts.

The price set on the account(s) is generally based on the amount of the monthly billing. Accounts are sold at anywhere from two to eight times the amount of gross monthly income they generate. Three to five times monthly billing is about average. In other words, it may cost you from $6,000 to $10,000 to purchase accounts which will give you a gross income of $2,000 a month.

If you want to go this route you should arrange to pay for the accounts over a period of months rather than up front. That way the jobs can pay for themselves as you go along and you won't risk any more money than you have to. The same considerations mentioned in regard to buying a business apply to purchasing individual accounts. Proceed with caution.

INVESTING IN A FRANCHISE

When you buy into a franchise you get a recognized name, training, advertising, a business plan and in some cases even the initial accounts — all for a substantial fee. You will usually be required to purchase your equipment from the franchisor. You may also have to pay an ongoing percentage (royalty) of your gross sales — anywhere from 3% to 10%.

If you are interested in franchise opportunities you should first take a look at the franchise directories available in your public library. Then contact the companies you are interested in directly. They will send you plenty of sales literature.

SUMMARY: Any of the above start-up alternatives involves considerable start-up capital and financial risk. Buying a business, purchasing janitorial accounts, or investing in a franchise without professional advice are risky propositions at best. Be sure to consult an attorney before signing any contracts or agreements.

CONSIDER YOUR OPTIONS

If you are new to this business you should thoroughly investigate starting your own service from scratch before attempting to buy your way in. Read this book carefully. Acquire as much information as you can from all available sources. Concentrate on how you could promote your service in your area. Apply initiative and creativity to your marketing program.

You will surprise yourself at how fast you can build a business of your own — then you will have the confidence and pride developed from doing it yourself! That is what this book is all about.

Chapter 3
SELLING YOUR SERVICE

The great thing about cleaning is that everyone needs your service. This is a "get up and go" business. You don't have to sit and wait patiently for customers to come to you. You can go out right now and create business for yourself. Opportunities to sell your service are everywhere.

To promote your business effectively, you need to be creative and get a number of selling methods working for you at once. This doesn't mean you need to spend a lot of money. There are many inexpensive ways to promote a janitorial service. In fact, some of the best promotional methods are the least expensive.

SELECTING YOUR MARKET

Your first step in promoting your business is to fix clearly in mind exactly what kind of accounts you want to concentrate on. Direct your promotional efforts toward those businesses, rather than attempting a shotgun approach at the whole field. If you want to service small to medium-sized office buildings, then they are your market. Go after them. Be specific — you don't want to waste valuable time, advertising and promotional materials on businesses that are not legitimate prospects for your service.

Locate every good prospect within the area you want to service by going through the Yellow Pages. Take a drive through the business areas of your town and write down the name and address of each building you would like to add to your accounts. Admittedly this is a lot of work, but the result will be a complete list of all possible commercial prospects.

As you go, make notes to yourself about each building. Any special information that could be included in your sales efforts just might make the difference. For instance, you may notice that the windows on a particular building are especially dirty, or that glass doorways are always covered in fingerprints. In your sales presentation you could mention something about your window cleaning expertise, or how window cleaning is a part of your regular service. If you plan to mail a form letter to a large number of businesses, you could include this special information on that one letter to personalize it. Be creative and make something happen.

If you are going after the residential market you will want to promote your services primarily to upper middle class and two-income families. These are the people who want and need your services and have the money to pay for them. You can locate these prospects physically by neighborhood or by renting professionally compiled mailing lists. Lists of homeowners are available by household income, address, occupation, new move-ins, professionals and executives, etc. Look in the phone book under the heading of "Mailing Lists".

REFERRALS OR WORD-OF-MOUTH ADVERTISING

The key to building a successful cleaning business is to do quality work and let your satisfied customers be your best advertisements. Good service is hard to find — if you can provide it you will be amazed at how fast your business will grow.

Referrals come automatically when you provide good service, but to get the most out of word-of-mouth advertising, you should be prepared to **encourage** it at every opportunity. For example, when you've completed a job and it is well done, the customer will usually remark on it. This is your opportunity to thank the customer, mention that you are looking for more work and hand out a few business cards or brochures. If you have a client who seems particularly satisfied, give him a handful. He will act as your salesman — no commission!

On the strength of a personal recommendation you can often set a higher price than your competitor and still get the job. There will always be low bidders but, with good references, you can compete against them at **your** price.

Once you have established a solid reputation you won't have to worry about getting enough work. You'll have so much you'll be hard pressed to keep up with it.

BUSINESS CARDS

Business cards are powerful little advertisements that can be distributed anytime, anywhere. Your card should have a professional appearance and indicate at a glance exactly what service(s) you are offering. Always keep a supply of business cards in your glove compartment and carry a few with you everywhere you go. You never know when a chance to promote your business will arise — pass out cards at every opportunity.

People usually save business cards, especially if they are attractive and well-designed. Include your card in any direct mail advertising you do. The prospect may toss out the sales letter but he or she will often slip your card into a file or desk drawer. You may get a call anytime, even years later.

SALES LETTERS

A sincere and well-written sales letter mailed to all your best commercial prospects can really bring results, especially when you follow up with a sales call or personal visit.

Writing an effective sales letter. Always write from the customer's point of view — show him how your service will save his time and money. Stress the quality and reliability of your work. Keep the letter relatively brief and direct. Use short sentences and paragraphs. If the client has to struggle to grasp your thoughts, he will simply throw the letter out.

Ideally you should write a personal, individual letter to each account you are cultivating. Of course, this is impractical if you are planning on sending out more than just a few letters. Save your customized letters for your very best prospects and develop a good form letter for the others. (See sample, next page)

Printing and mailing the letter. Type the form letter on your letterhead stationery, making sure it has the date on it. Don't let any spelling mistakes or poor grammar slip by.

Take it to a quick print shop and have it reproduced through offset printing, or use a top quality copy machine. Don't use a poor quality copier (like the ones in many post offices and libraries). Your letter won't look nearly as professional.

Include one or two of your business cards with each letter, along with your brochure or flyer if you have one. Be sure to sign each letter personally.

If you plan to make large mailings, you may want to inquire at your post office about getting a bulk rate permit. This will allow you to mail at a much lower cost. However, keep in mind that bulk mail is often considered "junk mail" and won't get opened by as many prospects.

FLYERS AND BROCHURES

Flyers and brochures can be excellent promotional pieces, but they must be professionally prepared to get the best results. First, get a basic idea of what you want your flyer or brochure to look like. Then take your ideas to a graphic artist for design and layout. Once you are satisfied with the artwork and design take it to a printer for offset printing.

MASTER

BUILDING MAINTENANCE

P.O. BOX 1087 • VALLEY CENTER, CA 92082

(619) 749-2380

April 15, 1989

The Parkway Building
1010 Business Street
Valley Center, CA 92082

Gentlemen:

I am writing to introduce you to my company, Master Building Maintenance. Our specialty is providing local businesses with top-notch janitorial service at reasonable rates.

We are equipped to expertly handle all of your maintenance needs, including professional window cleaning, carpet cleaning, hard floor care and "white glove" restroom service. Our company is fully insured and bonded for your protection.

Honesty, reliability and customer satisfaction are the keynotes of our business. We can offer many letters of recommendation from our customers, including the Valley National Bank just down the street from you.

I would appreciate the opportunity to meet with you and give you a free estimate of our services. Please call me at 749-2380 to discuss your maintenance needs.

Sincerely,

Frederick R. Massey
Owner

FRM:rm

SAMPLE SALES LETTER

Flyers — Flyers intended for soliciting residential work are usually done on 8½" x 11" sheets. Your printer can show you many different types of paper and colors of ink. Colored paper or ink costs a little more, but it is usually more effective than plain black on white.

You can distribute the flyers in selected neighborhoods and business districts, but not in the mail boxes — that's illegal. Flyers can also be inserted in your local paper or shopping guide, posted on bulletin boards or sent out as self-mailers.

Sales brochures — While a flyer is usually printed on an 8½" x 11" sheet, a sales brochure can be any size and may consist of several pages. The most economical type of brochure is a single page folded in thirds to fit inside a regular #10 envelope.

Sales brochures are valuable in soliciting commercial accounts. When making sales calls it is important to be able to leave something with the prospect. Your business card is good, but a business card **plus** a brochure is better. A brochure can be included with your sales letters and proposals, and can also be sent out as a follow-up to customers you contact over the telephone.

Your brochure need not be complicated or expensive. It should show your company name and logo (if you have one), tell what services you have to offer, your phone number and address and, of course, your "sales pitch". You will need to use your enthusiasm and creativity to find a sales angle that will work for you.

There is no doubt that writing good advertising copy is a challenge. One way to approach this is to visualize yourself explaining your business to a friend. How would you describe the service you provide? What makes you a little better or different than the "other guys"? Why should a customer hire you instead of XYZ company?

Remember, to make your sales brochure believable, you must **personalize** it. For instance, in your brochure you could show a picture of yourself along with a short personal note introducing yourself and your business. Or you could include a brief description of your business aims and ideals and finish off with your personal signature.

You don't need expensive, full-color printing on glossy paper to produce a quality look. If you use a colored paper with one color of ink you can achieve a quality appearance without having to pay for multi-color printing — for a quality appearance without having to pay for multi-color printing — for example, dark brown ink on cream colored paper, or navy blue ink on light blue paper.

PERSONAL SALES CALLS

One of the best ways to get commercial accounts is to call on local businesses personally. Just be yourself — you don't need an expensive suit or a polished speech. Walk into every business in your area and hand them your flyer or brochure. Say, "Hello, we just wanted to let you know about our service".

If you go into the right business at the right time you may be able to pick up an account on the spot. If they aren't interested or don't need your services at the present, you can still leave your business card and encourage them to give you a call if things change.

There is no question that if you make enough personal sales calls with a good appearance and a professional presentation you will get accounts. If you persevere, you can build up a substantial business volume in a short period of time.

You should keep an ongoing record of all your best prospects. This can be done with index cards or file folders. Each time you contact a prospect you can find out something new — who to contact, who is doing the cleaning now, in-house or contractor, etc. You can learn a lot this way about your competition and your local market.

TELEMARKETING

Telephone solicitation or "telemarketing" is an inexpensive way to reach prospective customers, but it takes persistence and lots of calls to get leads.

Telemarketing is well suited to selling residential services, such as carpet cleaning. People often notice that the carpet needs cleaning, but they just don't get around to doing anything about it. If you can catch them at the right time with the right sales pitch offering a "special in your area", you've got a good chance at getting their business. Of course you'll always get a lot more "noes" than "yeses", but don't take it personally — it's just a numbers game.

You can also use the telephone to **follow up** on your sales letters or personal sales calls, or to sell additional services to your present clients.

REMINDER ADVERTISING

Cleaning services should regularly mail reminder cards to their residential customers for such recurring work as window washing, floor waxing and carpet cleaning. This is an inexpensive and highly effective form of advertising. Reminder cards are a great way for service firms to generate repeat business.

Design a catchy reminder card and have a number of them printed up. When you complete a job, fill out a reminder card with the customer's name and address. File it chronologically, under the month when the work should be performed again. When that time comes just pick out the card and mail it. You will find that many customers will call and schedule the work the same day they receive your card. In this way you can establish a one-time customer as a regular client.

Another way you can encourage one-time customers to repeat is to offer a small discount if they will schedule the work on a regular basis. For example, instead of $75 for one time only, it will cost them $65 on a regularly scheduled basis.

NEWSPAPER ADVERTISING

Classified or display advertising in local daily and weekly newspapers can bring in lots of work. However, you've got to have the right ad in the right paper. The large daily city papers are usually not your best bet, because a classified or small space ad for a local service is often lost in the volume of print. If it isn't noticed on the first reading then it will probably be in the trash by the next day. In other words, your ad has a short life. In addition, half of the calls you do receive may be out of your service area.

Pick the newspapers you will advertise in carefully. Smaller local weekly papers and shoppers' guides can be great. And they are usually cheaper, so it won't cost you much to test them out with a small classified ad.

One good thing about newspaper ads is that they produce quick results. You know in a few days if your ad is working or not.

SPECIAL OFFERS

No matter what the advertising medium, a special offer can bring fast results, particularly in residential work. A special offer ad for a service business might take the form of a special low price or a coupon good for a discount. These are usually limited time offers. We've all seen this kind of ad — "10% off with this ad" or "1/3 off with this coupon". You can bet it works or businesses wouldn't keep doing it.

People are always on the lookout for a bargain. They clip these special offer ads and put them on a bulletin board or desk, where they serve as a daily reminder of your service. This greatly extends the life of your ad. Even if the person eventually throws your coupon out you have still accomplished something. Later on when the customer needs your service, your company name will come to mind.

Special offers are an excellent way for a new company to quickly build a clientele. When you offer a special you encourage new customers to give you a try. If you provide them with good service you will find that many of these new customers will become regular clients and refer other customers to you. In this way you can quickly develop a growing base of regular customers. Once you've done that you won't need to run any more specials.

> SPRING WINDOW CLEANING SPECIAL — Average 3 bedroom home $35 complete. Commercial and residential janitorial service. Quality work at reasonable rates. Master Building Maintenance, 749-2380.

YELLOW PAGE ADVERTISING

The Yellow Pages are a better advertising medium for some types of services than others. If your primary business is commercial janitorial service you may be surprised at how few clients you gain through the Yellow Pages. On the other hand, if you offer specialized services, residential cleaning or emergency services such as flood clean-up, a Yellow Pages ad may really pay off.

You should definitely have a **listing** in the Yellow Pages and perhaps a small ad, but don't overdo it. The Yellow Pages salesman will encourage you to spend your money on a big ad. He will point out some of the large ads taken out by your competitors — "You don't want to get left behind, do you?"

But if you are just starting out, you don't need or want a half-page ad in the phone book. Yellow Pages advertising is **expensive** and you must weigh the cost against your anticipated results. Remember, once you take out the ad you must continue to pay on it each month during the life of the directory, whether it is bringing in business or not.

If you want to try Yellow Pages advertising, start out with a smaller more affordable ad and see what results you get. If it seems to be bringing in business you can always expand to a larger ad in the next issue.

Don't overlook the small yellow page directories that are put out in many communities. These directories are less expensive and often target the specific area you want to service better than the large Yellow Pages. People often prefer to hire a local service and will look first in these community directories. This is particularly true if you are going after residential work.

Designing your ad — In a big city phone book your ad will be in direct competition with many others. It will need to be informative and well-designed to catch the reader's attention. To design your ad, you can use the Yellow Pages art staff, hire a professional graphic artist or do it yourself.

One way to stimulate creative advertising ideas is to visit the reference section of your local library. Most libraries have a collection of phone books for all the major cities in the U.S. Look in the Yellow Pages of different telephone books under the heading of "Janitor Service". In just a few minutes you'll get some great ideas for creating your own advertising.

Of course you don't want to copy anyone else's ad — rather, by studying a wide variety of "janitorial advertising", you will stimulate your own creative thinking.

MAGAZINES

In general, most magazines have too widespread a distribution to be of advertising use to a service business. However if there are **local magazines** in your area, they might be a good place to try a classified ad or a small space ad.

A local magazine has good potential for an ad promoting residential services because it has a concentrated local distribution. Your ad will have a considerable life span because the magazine is usually saved for a long time. It sits for months in doctors' waiting rooms, in barber shops and on coffee tables in thousands of homes. To test the effectiveness of advertising in a local magazine you can start with a small classified ad, then move up to a larger space ad if you see results.

SIGNS

Except in some unique situations, the only sign that you will use in the cleaning business is the vehicle sign on your work truck. Your vehicle sign serves as a constant and highly visible advertisement for your business. It gives you a lot of advertising exposure for the money.

Unless you are an expert painter, don't try to do your own truck lettering. A truck sign must be professional in appearance or it will do more harm than good. First get a basic idea of what you want your sign to look like, then hire a professional sign painter to do the actual lettering. Keep your truck sign simple — company name, telephone number (including area code) and the basic services you offer. Many companies start out with magnetic signs, which are less expensive than a permanent truck sign and can be transferred from one vehicle to another.

Whether you have a magnetic sign or a permanent truck sign you should make the most of it. When you go to do a job or make an estimate, park your truck right out in front where everyone can see it. After a while people will start to recognize your company name, and they will think of you when the subject of cleaning comes up.

TV AND RADIO

Radio and television have not generally proven to be good advertising media for maintenance companies. Some large residential cleaning companies and carpet cleaners use radio and TV, but for the new or smaller business the cost is prohibitive. You can use your money to greater advantage elsewhere.

SELLING TO CUSTOMERS WHO DO THEIR OWN CLEANING

Many prospective customers still take care of their own cleaning by using an "in-house" cleaning system. They hire and train their own custodians and buy and maintain their own cleaning equipment. Your challenge is to convince these in-house prospects to give contract cleaning a try.

Many businesses that use in-house janitors are not completely satisfied with the results. For example, when their janitor gets sick, goes on vacation or suddenly quits, they are stuck with trying to cover for him. This means they must hire temporary help or reassign a regular employee to do the cleaning.

When their vacuum breaks down they have to take it in to the shop and pay to get it fixed. And, unless they have back-up equipment, the carpet doesn't get vacuumed for several days. All of these cleaning-related problems are distractions from their regular business.

The way to approach customers who do their own cleaning is to show them how contract cleaning will benefit their overall operation. Why should they worry about cleaning schedules, crews and equipment, employee administration and supervision? It is an unnecessary and unprofitable burden. You can do the work better and for less money. When you take into consideration all the costs of running an in-house maintenance operation (including the owner's time), contract cleaning is usually a bargain.

Besides, cleaning is your specialty. You provide modern, specialized equipment and you maintain it. You have the know-how and the trained personnel to get the job done in the most efficient way. You provide all the employee supervision, benefits, insurance, hiring, recordkeeping and training. You take care of all these things at one set price. This frees the business owner and his employees to do their own special kind of work. You do what you do best; they do what they do best — and everyone benefits.

VACANCIES AND NEW CONSTRUCTION

Always keep your eye out for new construction and for businesses moving in to new quarters. You'll need to do a little detective work to find out who to talk to, but it will be worth your while. Inquire of building managers and general contractors. You may be the first one to show an interest in servicing their building.

When you are bidding on a newly constructed building, you should be able to negotiate an additional fee for the extra work involved in the initial clean-up. Once the new building is in shape it will be much easier to maintain than an older one.

A sample new construction sales letter is shown on the following page. Be sure to include several of your business cards with your letter. Then follow up with a phone call or personal visit.

SALES TECHNIQUES

Cleaning is not the kind of product people get excited about and buy impulsively. It takes time to cultivate good accounts. The best salesmen in this field take a low key approach and impress their clients with honesty and sincerity, rather than fast talk and hype.

Nowadays people are wary of the slick salesman. Everyone has been burned once too often. They are suspicious of hype, high pressure and smoothness. Be honest and straightforward — believable salesmanship.

MASTER

BUILDING MAINTENANCE

P.O. BOX 1087 • VALLEY CENTER, CA 92082

(619) 749-2380

May 1, 1989

Underhill Products, Inc.
1515 Main Street
Valley Center, CA 92082

Attn: Mr. Alvin Lee
        General Manager

RE: The Underhill Building
        100 First Avenue, Valley Center, CA 92082

Dear Mr. Lee:

We are writing to request the opportunity to submit a bid to provide janitorial services for your new office building currently under construction in Valley Center. We have seen the building going up and would like to introduce you to our company.

Since 1976 Master Building Maintenance has provided high quality janitorial service at affordable rates for businesses in this area. We have built our reputation on personal attention and consistent dependable service, as our customers will attest.

Our company is equipped to expertly handle every aspect of commercial maintenance, including window cleaning, carpet cleaning, hard floor care and "white glove" restroom service. We carry insurance and bonding for your protection and can offer a list of quality references.

We are particularly aware of the extra care and attention to detail required upon opening in a new building. When the time comes I would appreciate the opportunity to meet with you to inspect your new building and submit a free estimate of our services.

Thank you for your consideration.

Sincerely,

Frederick R. Massey
Owner

SAMPLE SALES LETTER

PUT YOURSELF IN THE CUSTOMER'S PLACE — In selling anything you must always try to determine the customer's point of view. Every situation is different and you will need to be alert to what each client is looking for. This doesn't mean you need a Master's degree in psychology! It's simply a matter of asking yourself two questions: "What are this client's real needs?" and "How can I convince him that my company can meet those needs the best?"

DEVELOPING CLIENT TRUST — More than any other factor, a successful professional cleaning business is built by development of client trust. People tend to buy things, whether it be automobiles, houses or janitorial services, from someone they like and feel they can trust. Keep in mind that the prospect you are talking to is considering turning over to you his keys, along with complete after-hours access to his office. You want him to have confidence in your ability and in the integrity of your character.

STRESS QUALITY — When you are just beginning you must make your newness work for you, rather than against you. Use your enthusiasm and imagination to generate interest in your quality-oriented cleaning company. It is important that you stress quality, dependability and personal attention, because they are what you have to offer. A newcomer can't advertise experience or point to an impressive list of accounts.

Be honest and enthusiastic when you talk with a prospective client. Tell him: "Yes, I'm just getting started, but I know what I'm doing and I guarantee that I'll give you 100%." You can go a long way with this attitude.

PLAN AHEAD so that you aren't caught off guard by questions and doubts that prospective clients may raise. Your sales success will depend in large part on your preparation. First, write down all the possible objections that a client might come up with. Think about how you could turn these negative suggestions into positive ones.

For instance, a client may question that a company of your size can handle his account — he was thinking of going with a larger outfit. Use this as an opportunity to stress the quality of your service and the personal attention that a small operation like yours can provide. With a little experience you will be able to anticipate a client's concerns and quickly set his or her mind at ease.

BE INFORMED — STUDY: In order to promote a janitorial service effectively you need to keep up-to-date on cleaning techniques and equipment. (See Chapters 9 through 12) Being well read and knowledgeable on the subject of cleaning will help your sales presentations greatly. When you know what you are doing, you can point out solutions to cleaning problems to a prospective customer. (See the Resources chapter for lists of books and trade magazines for professional cleaners.)

FOLLOW-UP — You must be systematic in your promotional efforts. Keep track of your results. Ask your customers how they heard of you and keep a record of how many responses or accounts each type of advertising brings in. Gradually you will see a pattern. Some promotions will work better than others. Find out what works for you and stick with it.

Important factors in your success in any promotional effort are repetition and timing. You have to keep trying until you **get your message to the right person at the right time.** For example, you may be working on a prospect for some time with no success. The client simply isn't interested right now. Your sales letters and promotional materials go straight in the trash. Then the day comes when the trash isn't emptied and the place is a mess — the janitorial service is slipping. Now this prospect is **interested** in what you have to offer and can be sold easily.

DON'T CRITICIZE YOUR COMPETITORS — There is a tendency among people in the service business to criticize other contractors. It may well be true that some of your competitors are bums, but criticizing them in front of a client is poor judgment. You will not win his respect this way. Put your best foot forward and let the customer judge for himself.

YOUR BUSINESS IS A REFLECTION OF YOU — Your promotional efforts, whether in person, by advertising, telephone or mail, should express your own personal enthusiasm and positive self-image. In the final analysis your business is a reflection of you, your thought and energy. Look at any successful business. You will see that behind it all is one person who applied creativity and determination to reach their goal.

Chapter 4
BIDDING AND ESTIMATING

Bidding janitorial work is not an exact science. No consultant or book can tell you exactly how much to charge for your service or for a particular job. It is up to you to weigh all the factors and come up with your best estimate. That is what competitive bidding is all about.

Several methods of estimating and pricing janitorial work are discussed in this chapter. There is no one "right" way to figure a bid price — the only "right" bid is the one that wins you the account and makes money for you.

In order for your bids to be consistently successful, they must:
1. Be competitive.
2. Provide for the desired level of services.
3. Cover all your costs of doing the work.
4. Generate your planned level of profit.

Bidding can become very complex and you can analyze and over-analyze a job until it becomes counter-productive. Keep your bid calculations simple and straightforward. You don't need a computer or a stack of complicated forms to bid the average janitorial account. Most bidding comes down to good judgment and common sense.

MAKING THE BUILDING INSPECTION

Once you have been asked to submit a bid, your first step is to make an appointment with the customer to look at the building in question. This is called the building inspection, building survey or walk-through. After you arrive at the job site, never just take a quick look around and give a price off the top of your head. It gives the impression of carelessness and overconfidence. In order to make an accurate bid you need to carefully inspect the building.

GATHERING THE FACTS ON THE PROSPECTIVE ACCOUNT

When you go to inspect the building, take along your clipboard or notebook and be prepared to take orderly notes. Everything that will affect your bid should be noted and written down. On small jobs a few notes may be sufficient, but on larger accounts you will need to be very systematic and detailed in your fact gathering. Remember once you leave the job site and go back to your office, you will have only your notes and your memory to go by.

First, make sure you've got all the basic facts on the prospective account written down — the building name and address, the person to contact, and his or her title and telephone number. Next, find out how often the client wants service and on which days. You must also find out what time frame the work must be accomplished in (for example, five day per week service, Monday through Friday, between the hours of 6 p.m. and 8 a.m.)

Next, inquire about the total square footage of the area you will be cleaning. If no accurate figures are available use a tape measure or a measuring wheel, or you can simply step it off. If you are calculating square footage by overall dimensions, be sure to subtract out a reasonable amount for uncleanable space, such as walls, partitions and areas not to be included in the cleaning contract. In addition to the overall square footage of the account, you will need to get measurements of the carpeted and tile floor areas separately. You may find it helpful to make a rough sketch of the building layout. Blueprints are rarely available on small accounts.

You should also ask about the number of people who work in the building. This will give you the information you need to determine **building density** (a major factor in estimating work time). The more crowded a building is, the longer it takes to clean.

Building density is the average number of square feet per building occupant, determined by dividing the total square footage of the building by the number of people who occupy the building. For example, a 10,000 square foot building with 50 occupants would have a density of 200 square feet per occupant. If no figures are available you can simply count the desks in each area as you do your walk-through. This will give you a "ball park" estimate of building population.

As you go from one part of the building to the next, try to visualize how the work would be performed. Are the areas open or congested? Are there elevators or will you have to go up and down stairs? Is there a storage closet for your supplies and equipment? Is there a source of hot water in the building? How far is the supply closet from the restrooms? Anything you notice that might speed up or slow down the work should be noted.

You also want to be sure not to throw your bid off by overlooking any work you will be responsible for. Be sure to inquire about any areas the client has not mentioned and don't assume anything, such as the size of the restrooms. Walk in and look them over. There might be ten fixtures in there instead of the usual four or five!

Pay particular attention to the present maintenance condition of the building. What condition are the floors, carpets and restrooms in? If the existing service is being terminated they have probably let things run down. You may be in for some hard work to get the account back in shape. Depending on the competition for the job, you will have to determine if you can ask for more money for the initial clean-up. (See page 76)

Be especially watchful for anything the client may say such as, "We are concerned about the appearance of the floor in the lobby area". These remarks are an indication to you of the things that matter to the client. These items should be specifically stated in your proposal and given special attention when you start the job itself.

Other account information you should make note of or ask about includes:
1. Alarm systems and security requirements.
2. Extra services desired by the client — outside cleaning, carpet cleaning, etc.
3. Restroom supplies — who will supply and pay for them?
4. Insurance and bonding requirements.
5. Special instructions from the customer.

DETERMINING THE RIGHT CLEANING SPECIFICATIONS

Cleaning specifications are the exact tasks required to clean the account, such as dusting, vacuuming, trash removal, restroom cleaning, etc. Often the owner is not really sure what cleaning tasks are required. He just knows that he wants his building clean and he doesn't want to pay a fortune for it.

If written cleaning specs are not available, then carefully write down all the information the client provides. Be sure to note the **frequency** of each task (how often it is performed). Then use your own knowledge of cleaning to draw up a set of specifications appropriate for the building. (For typical office cleaning specifications, see the examples on pages 86 and 87.)

When you write up specs you should take the customer's cleaning **budget** and cleaning **expectations** into account. Sometimes this can be a difficult area to evaluate. "Cleaning" is an intangible product and it means different things to different people. You will need to be observant and ask questions. Listen carefully to what the client has to say during the building survey to get a feel for what the situation calls for.

WORKING WITH CUSTOMER-SUPPLIED SPECIFICATIONS

In some situations the customer will supply you with a complete list of cleaning specifications. Customer-supplied specs have the advantage of uniformity — everyone is bidding on the same terms. Problems develop when the specifications supplied are inappropriate for the building. Sometimes the specs are just out of date, or they may have been written by someone with a limited knowledge of cleaning. Occasionally you will run into specs that have been copied from another building!

There are several ways of dealing with poorly written specifications. You can talk with the client and try to tactfully improve the specifications. Explain how a change in the cleaning specs could benefit the client.

For example, one of the customer's specifications may be "Shampoo all carpeting once a month". However, shampooing once a month will be costly, and the soap residue in the shampoo will cause the carpet to quickly become resoiled. In this situation you may want to suggest a carpet maintenance program which will call for daily vacuuming, regular spot cleaning, bonnet cleaning of traffic areas monthly and a deep cleaning (extraction) once a year, or as required. This change in the specifications could save the client considerable money, as well as improve the overall appearance of the carpet and prolong its life.

Sometimes it is not possible to work with the client on improving the specifications. In this case you can go ahead and bid the job as specified, or you can submit an alternative proposal based on your understanding of how the cleaning could be improved. If your alternative bid provides for a better cleaning program at a competitive price, it may well win out over other bidders who did not take the time or initiative to consider the client's best interests.

SELLING DURING THE WALK-THROUGH

There is much more to the building survey than just walking through making notes and recording facts. **This is the time to sell yourself and your company.** Your enthusiasm, confidence, professional manner and appearance all make their impression. This doesn't mean you need to wear a tux! Be yourself. A genuine manner will be far more effective in winning the client's confidence than fancy clothes.

Take a service-oriented attitude and strive to determine the customer's real maintenance needs. By taking an interest in the client and providing helpful information you can improve your chances of getting the job. Remember that the prospective customer is looking for someone he can **trust**.

Lastly, unless the job is small, don't speculate on price during the walk-through. If the customer asks for a price, explain that you will need some time to go over all the specifications and figures involved before you can determine a proper price for the service. Once you've completed the building inspection you should have all the information necessary to prepare your bid.

ESTIMATING JANITORIAL WORK TIME

Any good janitorial bid begins with an accurate assessment of the work time (man hours) required to do the specified work. This is because labor costs can represent up to 90% of your total cost of doing the work.

MAKING ROUGH TIME ESTIMATES

It is usually helpful to make rough estimates of work time as you survey the building. As you walk through, picture yourself actually doing the work and write down the time you estimate it will take to clean each area. These rough estimates can then be compared to your later calculations. Once you've developed a feel for estimating you will be surprised at how close your rough estimates come to the actual work time.

NOTE: You may want to first walk through the entire building to get an overall perspective on the account. Then go back and walk through each area again, taking a closer look and making your work time estimates.

CAN YOU USE STANDARD CLEANING TIMES?

Over the years many organizations have conducted time and motion studies to determine how long it should take to perform various cleaning tasks. Not surprisingly, the results of these studies often vary considerably.

To bid a job using standard cleaning times requires a complete physical inventory of all the items to be cleaned in the building. Standard times are then applied to each specific task or item to be cleaned (for example, "Clean ashtray – 15 seconds", "Dust picture frame – 10 seconds"). These times are then totaled and multiplied by the wage rate of the employee who will be performing the task. This gives you the total cost per task. Then all the total cost per task figures are added up to arrive at the total labor cost per month.

In theory, if the times assigned to each individual task are accurate and the inventory hasn't missed any items, then the total time arrived at should be close to the actual cleaning time. In practice, however, there are a number of difficulties involved in using standard cleaning times to price contract cleaning.

In real life bidding situations it is often not practical or possible to walk through each room counting every item (ashtrays, trash cans, telephones, bookcases, typewriters, file cabinets, etc.) On larger accounts this could take weeks!

Also, the process of cleaning is more than a certain number of tasks repeated one after the other. In addition to the actual time involved in performing each task, there is a great deal of in-between time, setting up, moving from one task to the next, traveling from one area to the next, etc. To estimate the **actual** cleaning time for the overall job requires that an allowance be made for this extra time — and this can be very difficult to determine.

Pricing janitorial work on an item-by-item basis is very time-consuming and requires stacks of paperwork. Due to the sheer volume of calculations and the possibility of mathematical errors, contractors who use this method have found computers extremely helpful. (See "Using Computers For Bidding Large Accounts" later in this chapter.)

On certain types of accounts (with the aid of a computer), an estimate based on standard cleaning times can produce an accurate bid. Generally speaking, though, this method of estimating cleaning time lends itself more to large in-house cleaning operations (hospitals, institutions, etc.) where there is time and staff available to conduct an item-by-item inventory and perform time and motion studies in a controlled environment.

JANITORIAL PRODUCTION RATES

A janitorial production rate is the average amount of square feet you can clean per hour in a particular type of building or area. For example, 3,000 square feet per hour is a "rule of thumb" production rate used by many contractors for estimating basic five day per week office cleaning. When you divide the square footage of an area to be cleaned by the correct production rate, you get the approximate number of hours required to clean the area. For example, 9,000 sq.ft. ÷ 3,000 sq.ft. per hour = 3 hours of cleaning time.

NOTE: For the purpose of estimating work time, buildings may be rated as "congested", "average" or "uncongested". Average density in office buildings runs about 150 to 200 square feet per occupant. Under 150 is starting to get congested and over 200 is considered uncongested.

On the following page is a list of average production rates for different types of accounts and cleaning tasks:

PRODUCTION RATE TABLE

SQUARE FEET CLEANED PER HOUR

Janitorial Service *	Congested	Average	Uncongested
Small offices (under 5,000 sq.ft.)	2500	2800	3000
Medium-sized offices (5,000-25,000 sq.ft.)	2600	3000	3400
Large office buildings (25,000+ sq.ft.)	2800	3400	4000
Manufacturing/Industrial offices	2000	2500	2800
Doctors' offices/Medical buildings	2500	2800	3200
Banks/Savings and loans	3000	3400	4000

*These production rates are "average" times for basic daily cleaning service (dusting, vacuuming, trashing and restroom cleaning) on carpeted accounts. For tile/hard floor accounts **subtract** 10% from the above production rates. These production rates do not include non-daily project work such as floor stripping, carpet cleaning or window cleaning. Production rates for these tasks are shown below.

Floor Maintenance Tasks			
Machine scrubbing (19" machine)	1200	2000	2400
Apply finish (one coat)	2500	3000	3500
Strip and refinish	—	—	400
Dry buffing (19" machine)	1700	2500	4000
Spray buffing (19" machine)	1500	2000	2500
High speed burnishing (20" machine)	—	—	15,000

Carpet Cleaning			
Surface cleaning (bonnet method)	750	1000	1250
Deep cleaning (extraction/steam)	500	750	1000

Window Cleaning (one side)			
Office windows (ground floor)	—	900	—
Office partitions	—	500	—
Store fronts	—	1800	—
Glass entry doors	—	600	—
Small panes (colonial style)	—	300	—

The above production rates are provided as **general guidelines** only. There are no exact production rates or cleaning times that fit every situation. Many factors affect how long it takes to clean a particular account.

FACTORS THAT AFFECT WORK TIME

Here are some of the factors you should take into consideration when estimating work time:

Building size — Generally you can achieve higher production rates in large buildings than you can in small ones.

Building density — Increased population in a building means more furniture to dust, more trash and ashtrays to empty, more traffic on the floors, heavier use of the restrooms and more obstructions to work around. Congested areas always take longer to clean than open ones.

Building condition — Older worn out buildings take longer to clean than new modern ones, and the results are never as satisfying.

Building design and layout — The number of stories, type of floors (carpet vs. tile), number of restrooms, elevators vs. stairways, etc. are all factors that affect cleaning time.

Building use — The kind of tenants in a building affects your cleaning time. For example, construction contractors' offices vs. law offices, or smoking vs. non-smoking offices. The amount of public use a building gets also affects your cleaning time, especially when restrooms are available to the public.

Cleaning frequency — A building you service daily can be cleaned faster (per square foot) than a building you service weekly. When you clean more frequently there is less dust and trash accumulated, and you get faster at the job.

Cleaning standard required — The level of service desired by the client is a major determinant of cleaning time. Do they expect "white glove" service, or do they just want the basics covered? The cleaning standard required should be determined during the building survey and outlined in the cleaning specifications in your proposal.

Equipment and supplies used — Using the right equipment and supplies for the job can have a big effect on the time it takes to clean. For example, you can vacuum uncongested areas quickly with a large vacuum, but in a highly congested area a smaller vacuum may get the job done faster.

Motivation and training of employees — A well-motivated employee who is trained in proper work techniques will work faster than the employee who is just "putting in time".

DEVELOPING YOUR OWN PRODUCTION RATES

Published tables of standard cleaning times and production rates have value as a starting point. They can serve as useful guidelines when you are just starting out. But the feedback from your own operations will always be much more useful to you.

As soon as possible you should start to time yourself and your employees and begin to develop your own production rates for each type of cleaning you do. **The production rates you generate from your own operations are the most valuable estimating and bidding tools you can acquire.**

After you start a new account you should check your actual work times against the times you had estimated when you bid the job. If you identify a significant difference between the estimated and actual work times, try to determine the cause so you can make the proper adjustments on your next bid.

Learn from your mistakes as well as from your successes. This is the best way to become more accurate in your estimating.

CALCULATING YOUR BID PRICE

There are many ways in which you can come up with a bid price. On very small jobs you can usually size up the work to be done and give your bid without the need for much detailed calculation. (See "Bidding — Shortcut Methods" and "Bidding Small Janitorial Accounts" later in this chapter.)

However, as you step up to larger accounts the need for a more exact method of determining your bid price becomes apparent. In order for your business to grow and be profitable, **all your costs plus your profit margin** must be built into each bid you make. The basic costs of providing janitorial service are:
1. Labor
2. Equipment and supplies
3. Vehicle costs
4. Miscellaneous direct costs
5. Overhead

ESTIMATING YOUR TOTAL MONTHLY LABOR COST

The first and most important task in any bid calculation is to estimate your labor cost. Cleaning labor (either yours or your employees) is the primary product you are selling — it is always your greatest cost. Labor costs should be calculated per month when the bid is stated as a monthly price. Here are the basic steps in calculating your total monthly labor costs for a bid:

1. First, estimate the number of man hours per day that will be required to clean the account. (Use your own experience, your own production rates or published time guidelines.) For example, if you are bidding a 6,000 square foot job and you apply a production rate of 3,000 square feet per hour, you would estimate a cleaning time of two hours per day (6,000 ÷ 3,000 = 2).

2. Next, multiply the total hours required to clean the account each day by the average number of days the account will be cleaned during the month. (See the table below.) This will give you the total **daily** man hours required to clean the account each month.

3. Now multiply the total daily hours per month by the wage rate you pay your employee and you will have the total direct labor cost per month of the daily cleaning.

4. Once you have determined the cost of the basic daily cleaning you can follow the same steps to determine the cost per month of any **non-daily** cleaning projects required at the account, such as window cleaning, floor waxing, carpet cleaning, etc. You can use the following table to determine the average number of days you will clean per month for various cleaning frequencies.

Cleaning Frequency	Days Per Month
7 days per week	30.42 days
6 days per week	26.0 days
5 days per week	21.67 days
4 days per week	17.33 days
3 days per week	13.0 days
2 days per week	8.67 days
weekly	4.33 days
every other week	2.17 days
monthly	1.0 days
every other month	0.5 days
quarterly	0.33 days
every 4 months	0.25 days
semi-annually	0.17 days
annually	0.08 days

5. Next, total the daily cleaning cost and non-daily (project) cleaning costs. This will give you your total **direct** labor costs per month.

NOTE: On larger accounts several employees in different wage brackets may be working various hours on the account (such as janitors, lead men, route supervisors, waxers, etc.) In this case simply determine the hours per month each employee or supervisor will spend on the job and multiply by their respective wages. Then total these amounts.

6. Now estimate your **indirect** labor costs. Indirect labor costs consist of payroll taxes, Workmen's Compensation insurance, liability insurance and employee benefits.

Payroll tax rates are mandated by federal and state laws. Current rates are available in circulars published by the IRS and your state tax office. Insurance costs vary depending on the benefits you offer and the rates you are able to obtain. Your insurance agent will have exact rate information for your type of business and area.

Indirect labor expenses are a major cost of doing business. They can add as much as 30% to the base wage you pay. For example, if you pay one part-time employee $100 a week, it is actually costing you up to $130 a week in total payroll. This is often overlooked when computing labor costs for a bid. For more information on these employer expenses, see pages 122 to 124.

7. Finally, add your direct labor cost to your indirect labor cost and you have your **total monthly labor cost**.

ESTIMATING EQUIPMENT AND SUPPLIES COST

Many contractors use 6% to 9% of the monthly labor cost as a "rule of thumb" factor for estimating the cost of equipment and supplies (6% for carpeted accounts, 9% for hard floor jobs). These figures are based on national averages.

Supplies — Cleaning supplies are the products you use up each day in the course of servicing your accounts (floor finish, detergents, dust cloths, etc.) Usually it is not worth your while to estimate the cost of every small item of supplies individually. However if the job you are bidding on requires large scale floor maintenance, you may want to estimate the cost of expensive supplies like floor finish, sealer or restorer on an item-by-item basis.

The amount of floor care products you will need can be easily estimated by dividing the total square footage of the floor by the estimated product coverage (listed on the product label). Once you know how many gallons you will need per month, just multiply by the price per gallon and you'll have your monthly bid cost.

Equipment —The term equipment refers to assets with a useful life of one year or more (buffers, vacuums, etc.) Equipment cost is usually not a major factor on the individual bid, because equipment costs are written off over a number of years (the "useful life" of the equipment).

To estimate equipment costs in detail, take the total purchase price of the equipment and divide by its useful life (usually five or seven years). Then divide that figure by 12 to get the monthly cost for your bid.

For example, if you buy a $1,000 machine with a life of five years, your calculation will look like this: $1,000 ÷ 5 years ÷ 12 months = $16.67 equipment cost per month.

When equipment is used on more than one account the monthly cost should be prorated, based on the estimated percentage of use the equipment will get on the account you are bidding. Using the same example, if the $1,000 floor machine is going to be used on the account 25% of the time, you would multiply $16.67 by 25% to get the amount that should be included in your monthly bid price ($16.67 x 25% = $4.17).

ESTIMATING VEHICLE COSTS

The easiest way to calculate vehicle costs is to estimate the **additional** miles your company vehicle(s) will need to drive to service the new account each month. Then set a flat rate per mile which will cover all the costs of operating the vehicle (gas, oil, insurance, depreciation, etc.) One rate often used is the IRS standard mileage rate of 24¢ per mile.

Vehicle costs should only be included in your bid when you use your car or company vehicle in servicing the account. When your employees or supervisors use their own cars, vehicle expense will not apply (unless you pay them a mileage allowance).

Vehicle costs are normally a minor factor in estimating, but they can become a major consideration when you are bidding on a remote job. Remember, even when you hire a local crew, a good deal of travel time will be required in checking up on the account, running back and forth delivering supplies, picking up keys, handling complaints and keeping the client happy. If the job is to be profitable, these transportation costs should be anticipated and built into the price.

ESTIMATING MISCELLANEOUS DIRECT COSTS

On some accounts you will have special costs not covered elsewhere. Here are two examples:

1. **Subcontracts** — When you plan on subcontracting portions of a job, you should get firm bids from your subcontractors **before** submitting your bid and then add this expense into your bid price.

2. **Restroom supplies included in the contract** — Sometimes a client will want restroom supplies (hand towels, toilet tissue, soap, etc.) **included** in the contract price, rather than billed for separately. Paper products are expensive and waste is hard to control. Providing these supplies can add as much as 20% to your monthly cost of doing the work.

NOTE: Whenever possible, paper products should be separated from the bid price and billed back to the client. (See page 101)

DETERMINING YOUR TOTAL OPERATING COSTS

When you add up your labor expense, equipment and supplies expense, vehicle costs and miscellaneous direct expenses, you have your **total operating costs** of handling the account. Now all that remains is to include an allowance in your bid for overhead expense and profit.

ESTIMATING OVERHEAD EXPENSE

Overhead is the general cost of doing business — postage, telephone, advertising, utilities, license fees, etc. These are all the expenses which are not directly connected to any one account. (In other words, if you lost an account these expenses would still be there.) In order to stay in business and make a profit, your bids must include an allowance to cover these indirect expenses.

To determine how much you are actually spending on overhead, go to your expense journal and add up all the overhead expenses for the last year. Then divide this figure by your gross business income for the same period.

This will tell you what percentage of your total income you are spending on overhead. You can use this percentage to budget overhead for each new account you bid. (See "Mark-Up Method" on the next page.)

NOTE: If you are just starting out and have no experience to go by, you can use 7% as a starting point for estimating your overhead.

Overhead can vary substantially from one company to the next. This is one area where the small contractor can have a decided advantage. While a large company may have to allow 15% to 20% for overhead expense, a small, home-based business may be able to get by with as little as 5% to 10% overhead expense.

PROFIT MARGIN

Profit is the most important part of any bid. This is your reason for being in business! How much profit you can include in your bid (and still be competitive) depends on many factors, including the competition, the type and size of the account and your relationship with the client.

Some of your large competitors operate with profit margins as low as 2% or 3%, but you will need much more than that. As an owner/operator of a small, low-overhead company your profits can range anywhere from 10% to 50%, or even more. A profit margin of 20% to 30% is a reasonable goal for a small, streamlined cleaning company handling quality accounts.

MARK-UP METHOD

Your profit margin on an account is usually calculated as a percentage of the total bid price. For instance, if you make a $200 profit on a $1,000 account, your profit margin is 20%.

Since overhead is also calculated as a percentage of the total bid price, these two bid factors can be marked up together. For example, if your overhead percentage is 10% and you want a 20% profit margin, you would need to include a mark-up of 30% in your bid price to cover these two bid factors.

This means that your total operating costs for the account must equal 70% of your bid price. (70% operating costs + 30% profit & overhead markup = 100% bid price). In order to calculate a bid price that includes a mark-up of 30%, you need to **divide your total operating costs by 70%.**

For example, if you estimate that your total operating costs will be $800 and you want to mark the price up by 30%, your calculation would look like this: $800.00 ÷ 70% = $1,142.85 (total bid price). Your profit and overhead margin on this job would be $342.85, which is 30% of your total bid price.

To calculate a markup of 35%, you would divide your total operating costs by 65%. For a markup of 20%, divide your operating costs by 80%, and so on.

BID CALCULATION SUMMARY

The basic steps in calculating a reliable bid are:

1. Estimate your total monthly labor cost — add together your total direct labor cost plus your payroll costs.

2. Estimate your equipment and supplies costs — use a percentage of the total monthly labor cost, or make an item-by-item estimate.

3. Estimate your vehicle costs — use a flat rate per mile.

4. Add in any other miscellaneous direct costs that apply to the job, such as subcontracts or restroom supplies included in the contract, etc.

5. Determine your total operating costs by adding the total monthly labor cost, equipment and supplies cost, vehicle costs and any miscellaneous costs.

6. Arrive at your monthly bid price by marking up for overhead and your desired profit.

The completed bid work sheet on the next page shows how each of these steps is applied in an actual bid.

BIDDING — SHORTCUT METHODS

THE TWO TIMES MARK-UP

The two times mark-up is a "rule of thumb" bidding method used by many cleaning contractors to produce quick, reliable bids. To use this method you simply estimate your total labor cost per month and **double it**. For example, if you estimate total labor costs of $400 a month, you would charge $800 a month for your service (2 x $400).

The two times mark-up covers all your direct operating costs, overhead and profit. Many small cleaning contractors use this method because it is fast, easy and efficient. On the average account, doubling your labor cost will give you a profit margin of between 18% and 30% (depending on your actual operating costs).

The two times mark-up is especially useful for making quick estimates on small jobs, where a full scale cost breakdown is not justified. The main drawback to this method is that it will not necessarily produce the lowest possible bid. Also, a straight two times mark-up over labor costs may not be geared to your own profit goals.

BID WORK SHEET

BID FOR __VALLEY NATIONAL BANK__ DATE __4-10-89__

ADDRESS __1001 1ST. AVE. VALLEY CENTER, CA 92082__ BID BY __F. Mauer__

AREA & TASK	SQUARE FOOTAGE	÷ SQ. FEET PER HOUR	= HOURS PER DAY	× DAYS PER MONTH	= HRS. PER MONTH	× WAGE RATE	= MONTHLY COST
GENERAL CLEANING	6000	3400	1.76	21.67	38.13	$ 4⁵⁰	$ 171.58
STRIP & REWAX LOBBY	600	400	1.5	.33	.5	5⁰⁰	2.50
CLEAN WINDOWS	1800	800	2.25	.5	1.125	7⁰⁰	7.88

Cleaning Frequency	Days Per Month
7 days per week	30.42 days
6 days per week	26.0 days
5 days per week	21.67 days
4 days per week	17.33 days
3 days per week	13.0 days
2 days per week	8.67 days
Weekly	4.33 days
Every other week	2.17 days
Monthly	1.0 days
Every other month	0.5 days
Quarterly	0.33 days
Every 4 months	0.25 days
Semi-annually	0.17 days
Annually	0.08 days

TOTAL DIRECT LABOR COST $ 181.96

PAYROLL COSTS $ 45.50

TOTAL MONTHLY LABOR COST $ 227.46

EQUIPMENT AND SUPPLIES COST $ 18.20

VEHICLE COSTS $ 32.00

OTHER COSTS $ —

TOTAL OPERATING COSTS $ 277.66

OVERHEAD AND PROFIT $ 119.00

TOTAL MONTHLY BID PRICE $ 396.66

SAMPLE BID WORK SHEET

HOURLY RATE

Bidding at an hourly rate is a shortcut method used by many small contractors who do the work themselves. To use this method you simply estimate your time per cleaning, multiply by the number of times you clean per month and multiply that amount by the hourly rate you want to earn. For example, if you estimate a job will take you two hours per night, five nights a week, and you want to earn $12 per hour, your bid calculation would look like this: 2 hours x 21.67 days x $12 = $520.08 monthly bid price.

NOTE: When you use this method of pricing your service you are not actually getting paid by the hour. You are just using an hourly rate to figure your bid price.

The hourly rate bid is most often used by one man companies and small contractors who do some or all of the cleaning themselves. There is nothing wrong with this method of bidding. It is simple, straightforward and effective. However, in pricing your service this way you must remember that you will often be bidding against companies that use employees — their price is going to be based on labor expense plus a mark-up.

In highly competitive bidding situations (where price is the major factor), you will need to keep your hourly rate between $8 and $15 an hour to be competitive. If you go much higher you will be "out of the ball park" on most competitive bids. Remember, even though your competitors have to charge for more overhead, they also pay their janitors low wages. So even after marking up their labor they are usually charging around $8 to $12 an hour for basic janitorial service.

If you run a small cleaning company and you do the work yourself, you should stay away from the type of accounts that always go to the lowest bidder. You'll wind up wasting your time and energy in unprofitable work.

PRICE PER SQUARE FOOT

Pricing basic janitorial work by the square foot is a shortcut bidding method used by many experienced contractors.

To use this method you simply measure the area to be cleaned and multiply the total square footage by a flat rate per square foot. For example, if you are bidding a 5,000 square foot bank and you want to charge 7¢ a square foot, your monthly bid price would be $350 (5,000 x .07 = $350).

Although bidding by the square foot sounds simple, it isn't. To be accurate the price you charge per square foot must cover all your costs of doing the work, as well as provide your profit margin. Among the factors that will affect your costs of doing the work are wage rates, level of service desired, frequency of cleaning, type and size of account, condition of the building, building density, building use, competition, geographical location, etc. Trying to set a flat rate per square foot to cover all of these variables is no easy chore.

Bidding by the square foot works best in bidding situations where the cleaning requirements are fairly standard, such as basic five day per week office cleaning. The trick is to be able to identify factors in individual buildings which will affect your basic rate per square foot, and then adjust your price per square foot up or down to compensate. This takes a good deal of experience both in estimating and in doing the work.

The obvious advantage of bidding by the square foot is that you can go quickly from the square footage of the building to the final price. The big disadvantage is that when you apply a flat rate per square foot it covers so many cost variables that there is a much greater possibility of error. Bidding by the square foot is not necessarily the best or most reliable method for someone new to the business.

Because of all the factors that can affect the price per square foot, it is usually best to first calculate your bids using estimates of your actual costs. Then use the price per square foot as a way of double checking your bid rather than as a bidding method in itself.

DOUBLE CHECKING YOUR BID PRICE

You can use the price per square foot to check your proposed bid price, to see if it falls within a competitive range for the type and size of building you are bidding. In this case you calculate your price per square foot **after** you figure your bid price.

To do this simply divide your bid price by the number of square feet in the building. For example, if your proposed bid price is $600 and the account is 10,000 square feet, your price per square foot per month would be 6¢ ($600 ÷ 10,000 = .06). If the price per square foot you come up with is not in line with the local "going rate", it may be an indication that you have made an estimating or mathematical error somewhere along the way.

WHAT IS THE "GOING RATE"?

You will hear professional cleaners mention prices ranging anywhere from 4¢ per square foot to 20¢ per square foot per month. But to be able to compare and make sense of any price per square foot figures, you need specific information on the account — the size of the building, the wage rates, the cleaning frequency and all the other factors that affect the cost of doing the work.

The size of an account has a lot to do with how much you can charge per square foot. For example, depending on your area, you may be able to charge $175 a month to clean a 1,200 square foot office. This works out to 14.6¢ per square foot. Meanwhile, just down the street, you may have a 25,000 square foot office building which you clean for $1,500 a month, or 6¢ per square foot.

Here are some average price ranges for basic five day per week janitorial service:

AVERAGE PRICE PER SQUARE FOOT PER MONTH

Large office buildings (over 25,000 sq.ft.)	4-5¢
Medium-sized office buildings (10,000-25,000 sq.ft.)	5-7¢
Small office buildings (3,000-10,000 sq.ft.)	6-8¢
Banks	6-9¢
Medical offices	7-9¢
Very small offices	8-20¢ *

* On very small jobs or accounts you service less than five days per week, the price per square foot will vary so widely that it is not a reliable indicator for estimating.

Keep in mind that these are **general price ranges only**. How much you can charge per square foot on any particular account depends on many factors that apply to your own situation, such as competition, local wage rates and the general economic conditions in your area.

LOW BIDDING

In the janitorial business there are always low bidders who set a price solely with the intention of undercutting everyone else. Then they cut corners to try and make up the difference. But you can't build a reputation or a business that way — not a good one at least. Fortunately, many clients are wise to low bidders.

There are times when a lower than usual bid makes sense. For example, in a multi-tenant building you can sometimes get your foot in the door with a low bid on the basic janitorial service, then make your money by selling more profitable specialized services to the tenants.

Or you may come across a potential customer who is in a position to give you a lot more work in the future. In this case you may want to give them a special price on the first job to show what you can do, and to get the inside track on more work. But for the most part, bidding below the profit level you need is a mistake.

When you bid too low you get hard work and low pay, definitely not the goal of self-employment! If you are just starting out, don't be reluctant to charge a fair price for your services. We're not in this business to scrape by!

BIDDING SMALL JANITORIAL ACCOUNTS

Bidding a small account is usually a very informal process. Many small accounts tend to hire on the spot and expect immediate service. Sometimes the key question they have for you is "Can you start tonight?"

On small accounts you can almost always charge more per square foot, and make more money per hour, than you can on larger jobs. There are several reasons for this:

1. There is **less competition** — Most of your larger competitors are concentrating on the big office buildings downtown. They are doing a large volume business and it just isn't cost effective for them to hire, train and supervise janitors to do small jobs and route work.

2. Small accounts often select a janitorial service on a **personal basis**. It usually comes down to who can sell himself or herself the best, rather than who has got the rock bottom price. In other words **who you are** and how people feel about you often counts for more than the lowest bid. On small accounts a personal referral and word of mouth often outweigh minor price differences.

3. When you get down to the very small accounts, you can pretty much throw the conventional bidding formulas out the window. This is because you are getting into a price range where a **minimum charge** starts to take effect.

For example, even if a once a week job only takes 20 minutes per cleaning you will want to charge at least $10 to $15 a visit as a minimum charge to cover travel time, set-up time and the miscellaneous costs of handling the account. This is why you will often wind up making $25 or more per hour and more than 10¢ per square foot on small janitorial accounts.

The key to making good money on small janitorial accounts lies in developing a number of small highly profitable jobs into a **geographically concentrated route**. Once you have an account, identify all the nearby prospects. Stop by these local businesses in person, send them a sales letter or give them a call using the original account as a reference. It always costs less to service nearby accounts once you've made the arrangements to handle the first one. Be sure to bring this fact out in your sales presentation. Once you establish a route of these small profitable accounts you've got yourself the start of a beautiful little business.

NOTE: A one page bid form such as the one shown on pages 81 and 82 is ideal for bidding small janitorial accounts. This form can be quickly filled in at the job site and submitted to the customer for immediate approval and acceptance.

BIDDING LARGE JANITORIAL ACCOUNTS

There is no simple or shortcut method for calculating a reliable bid on a large scale job. The larger the account the more time and care is required to gather all the facts needed to make an accurate bid.

Remember that any errors you make in estimating will be magnified. For example, if you are 10% off on a $500 bid, it will cost you $50 — no big deal. But on a $5,000 a month job, a 10% error will cost you $500. You've got to spend the necessary time to make a detailed building survey and take a close look at all your costs.

SURVEYING A LARGE ACCOUNT

In surveying a large multi-story building it is usually best to start from the top floor and work your way down, considering each floor individually as if it were a separate job. By breaking the account down into manageable units it is easier to visualize the actual cleaning that needs to be done.

On larger buildings, blueprints or floor plans are usually available. These can help you to get a handle on the layout and size of different areas in the building. The fastest way to get the measurements in a large building is to use a sonic measuring device.

Plan on spending some time and walking through the building several times. The more you know about the prospective account the better off you'll be, both in bidding the job with confidence and handling the work once you're in the building.

BIDDING YOUR FIRST LARGE ACCOUNT

Never bid a large account using any type of flat rate or shortcut bidding method. Always do a full scale cost evaluation. (See pages 61 through 67) You can lose your shirt bidding large accounts by the square foot without considering your actual costs of doing the work. For example, on a 100,000 square foot building the difference between a bid of 4.1¢ a square foot and 4.9¢ a square foot is $800 a month, or $9,600 a year.

Beginners should first gain experience in both cleaning and estimating, and develop their own production rates, before attempting to bid large scale janitorial work.

Here are a few important points you should consider before going after your first large account:

1. **Increased competition** — When you go after large accounts you step into a whole new competitive arena. Large volume contractors operating with low profit margins are concentrating on these accounts. This competition forces the price down.

Low profit margins make for very tight bids and low prices per square foot. The smaller contractor should carefully consider if this is the kind of work he wants.

2. **Increased production rates** — Contractors who are used to bidding smaller office buildings at 2,500 to 3,000 square feet per hour often overbid the larger accounts. This is because they are competing against companies that are geared up to clean large buildings at higher production rates, of 3,500 to 4,000 square feet per hour and more.

In fact, by utilizing modified cleaning specifications, specialized equipment and team cleaning systems, some experienced contractors are able to achieve production rates of up to 6,000 square feet per hour in large office buildings.

3. **Initial equipment and supplies costs** — The initial investment in new equipment and supplies required to gear up for a large scale job can be substantial. At the very least you'll need several new vacuums, some rolling trash cans and a few fully-equipped maid carts.

Large scale hard floor accounts require the highest initial investment of all. You'll need automatic scrubbers and high speed burnishers — a major outlay of cash. Few beginners are ready to tackle these accounts (especially if you are starting from scratch).

4. **Cash flow** — It takes money in the bank to finance the start-up of a large account. You will have several payrolls to meet before you see your first month's check. There will be initial equipment and supplies costs; you may need to increase your insurance coverage and your payroll costs will go up.

For example, consider your "basic" 100,000 square foot office building. It will take a crew of four men about eight hours a night to clean this account. If you pay three full-time janitors $4.50 an hour and a lead man $5 an hour, you will have a nightly payroll of $148, or $740 a week.

Even if the account pays you on time, you will have to meet five or six weekly payrolls before you see any money from the job. That works out to $3,700 to $4,440 out of pocket, plus another $1,000 or so for payroll expenses, plus another $500 to $1,000 for new equipment and supplies. That puts you roughly $5,200 to $6,500 into the job before you get your first month's payment.

It always takes several months to get your cash flow turned around on a large janitorial account. And if your big account is a slow payer — watch out!

All this is not meant to discourage you, but to let you know what you are getting into when you bid on your first large account. It is not something you can jump right into. You've got to work up to it. Until you've got enough experience, capital and cash flow behind you, you will be better off concentrating on accounts of a more manageable size (under 25,000 square feet). Your start-up costs per account will be much lower and you can add the smaller accounts without putting such a strain on your operations and finances.

Once you've built a strong foundation of small profitable accounts you will be in a better position to go after the large jobs if you want them.

USING COMPUTERS FOR BIDDING LARGE ACCOUNTS

Because of the sheer volume of calculations and factors to be considered, some contractors who specialize in large accounts are now using computers to handle the number crunching.

Several companies offer specialized software for bidding and estimating contract cleaning. These programs, generally referred to as "workloading programs", will compute your labor hours and costs by using pre-established standard times. Or you can input your own production rates into the computer memory. Once all the data from the building survey has been keyed in, the computer can make all the calculations at electronic speed.

Based on the information you key in, the computer will generate a detailed printout showing tasks, time per tasks, frequency, hours per month, costs per month, etc. Your printout may then be used as part of your proposal to help impress the client.

By changing any of the job variables you can quickly change the entire estimate. You can calculate alternative prices, using different cleaning frequencies, specifications, wage rates or whatever combinations of variables you desire. Also, based on the information you key in, the computer can generate a complete price quotation at whatever level of profit you indicate. This speed and flexibility in working with the variables can be very useful when bidding large accounts.

However, it must be remembered that a computer-generated bid will only be as accurate as the information you key in. If you input your own proven production rates the bid is more likely to be accurate than if standard times are used.

Specialized software for bidding and estimating janitorial work is not sold over the counter in local computer stores. There are only a few sources of this highly specialized software and each system will not run on all personal computers.

Several sources of bidding software for cleaning contractors are listed in the Resources chapter. For exact details on what they have to offer you should write or call each company. Be forewarned — some of these products are expensive!

HANDLING INITIAL CLEAN-UP EXPENSE

Initial clean-up is an important cost factor often overlooked on many jobs. There are two situations which you will run into — buildings where the cleaning has been neglected and new construction clean-up. (Although the general contractor is ordinarily responsible for construction clean-up, this is usually just rough cleaning and leaves the building far short of being ready for regular maintenance service.)

In either of these two cases, a major clean-up will be required before you can start the regular maintenance service. This is going to cost you time and money. In fact, the cost of initial clean-up can often exceed the first month's payment on the contract. How do you handle this initial clean-up expense? Basically, you have three options:

1. **Absorb the cost** — Do it for free. Unfortunately all too often the contractor winds up doing the initial clean-up for free. The extra work is simply considered part of the process of getting the new account, a sort of necessary evil. When the cost is absorbed by the contractor the job becomes less profitable than it should be.

2. **Prorate the expense** — Estimate how much the initial clean-up will cost and prorate the expense over the first year (or over the expected life) of the

contract. This way you get paid for the work eventually, even though your expense is all up front. The problem here is that adding the initial cost into your contract price may make your bid too high.

3. **Request a one-time initial clean-up fee** — This is usually the best approach, but you must sell the client on the need for and importance of this initial clean-up. One way to request an initial clean-up fee is to mention it in your proposal cover letter. For example, say: "Should you decide to proceed under this proposal there will be a one-time fee of $100.00 for initial clean-up."

RESIDENTIAL ESTIMATING

Residential cleaning work is usually obtained on a much less formal basis than commercial work. You run into a great many one-time jobs and referrals, and verbal agreements are common. Generally the prospective customer contacts your office by telephone. Depending on the work required, you can either give a price over the phone or make an appointment to give an estimate.

If it is a one-time, small job and the work is fairly standard (for example, cleaning the windows in a one-story tract home), give a price over the phone. You don't want to spend time and money driving around giving estimates. But be sure to indicate that if there are any unforeseen complications you will need to charge more. Tell the customer that you will confirm the price when you arrive to do the job, before you start work.

For large residential jobs, such as major floor cleaning (stripping, refinishing, etc.) you will need to see the job before you can give a price. These estimates can be given verbally or handwritten on a simple one page estimating form. Try to group your appointments. If you can do all the estimates in one area on one trip it will save you time and driving. If you only have one estimate to give, then schedule it to fit into your regular work or supervising route.

The big advantage of residential cleaning, especially if you are just starting, is that you get paid on the spot — a real help to your cash flow.

ESTIMATING RESIDENTIAL CLEANING TIMES

As in the commercial field there are no exact time standards you can rely on. In fact, there are probably more factors that can affect job time in residential cleaning than in commercial.

For instance, you can say that it takes one hour to clean 1,000 square feet of glass. But how long does it take to clean 1,000 square feet of glass in a home? You may find yourself leaning around fish tanks and curtains and climbing over sofas, all the while being careful not to step on toys, kids, cats and plants.

Here are some sample times from typical residential cleaning jobs. Remember, the work always goes much faster when you are familiar with the particular job.

RESIDENTIAL CLEANING TIME GUIDELINES

<u>Estimated Times</u>

<u>Light Housecleaning</u>
     Average 1,200 sq.ft. home
Vacuuming, dusting, spot cleaning
General cleaning of bathrooms   1 person 3½ – 4 hrs.
and kitchen   2 people 1½ hrs.

<u>Heavy Duty Housecleaning</u>
     Average 1,200 sq.ft. home
Carpet vacuumed and shampooed or
steam cleaned.
Draperies vacuumed.
Tile floors stripped and waxed.
Windows cleaned, inside and out.
Kitchen: Walls wiped down, oven and
refrigerator cleaned.
Bathroom: Shower cleaned, sinks, toilets,
walls wiped down, medicine cabinet
cleaned, floors mopped.   2 people 4 – 6 hrs.

<u>Apartment Cleaning</u>
     650 sq.ft., vacant
General clean-up   2 people 1 – 1½ hrs.

<u>Scrub and Wax Tile Floor</u>
     400 sq.ft. kitchen—dining room floor.
Move furniture.
17" floor machine   1 person 1 – 1½ hrs.

Window Cleaning

      Average 1 story single family residence
2 to 3 bedrooms, modern windows
Clean inside and out – 16" squeegee   1 person 1½ – 2 hrs.

Carpet Cleaning

      1,500 sq.ft. home
Steam cleaning
Move small furniture   2 people 1½ – 2 hrs.

PRICING RESIDENTIAL JOBS

Residential cleaning rates vary from one area to the next. One way to get an idea of professional housecleaning prices in your area is to call several local companies and ask for an estimate on your home. Or ask friends and relatives who have used local services what they have paid.

Ten to twenty dollars per hour of work time is an average price range for professional housecleaning. But whatever you do, don't charge your customers for service by the hour. **Charge by the job.** Some homeowners resent it when they find out you are making more money per hour than they are!

Considering the travel and set-up time involved in residential cleaning, you may find it necessary to charge a minimum fee per job. Depending on your area, a minimum charge of between $25 and $45 would be appropriate.

If you offer specialized services like carpet cleaning, floor care or window cleaning, you can charge much more per hour than you can for general cleaning. For example professional carpet cleaners with truck-mounted equipment are charging between 10¢ and 30¢ a square foot (depending on their area) for residential carpet cleaning. At production rates of 500 to 1,000 square feet per hour, that works out to good money!

Chapter 5
BUILDING MAINTENANCE PROPOSALS

If there is one thing that holds people back from starting a janitorial business, it is the belief that there is some secret format for the contract paperwork, known only to insiders. This uncertainty keeps many otherwise qualified individuals from getting a start in professional cleaning.

When a person first thinks about going into this business, a number of basic questions come to mind. What goes into a proposal? How is it set up? What's the difference between a bid and a proposal? Where does the contract come in? If they cannot find answers to these key questions, many people are afraid to attempt contracting. They know how to do the work, but not the paperwork.

THE PROPOSAL

In the janitorial business the proposal is often the only paperwork signed by both parties. It is drafted to serve as the bid and contract rolled into one. Here's how this works: your bid is the price set in the proposal. When the customer accepts this price, he signs and agrees to the terms and conditions set forth in the proposal. When the proposal has been signed by both client and contractor, it becomes the contract.

There is no "standard" janitorial contract or proposal format in use in the cleaning industry. There are many different ways you can package your bid, but the two formats most frequently used by cleaning contractors are the **preprinted form** and the **customized letterhead proposal**. The type of proposal you use will depend on the job you are bidding. Each account is different and during the initial interview and building survey you will usually be able to determine which format would best sell the job.

ONE PAGE BID FORM

On many jobs you can submit your bid on a one page bid form, such as the one shown on the next page. Often small accounts do not need or expect a customized letterhead proposal. Not only is the expense and preparation time not justified, but the effect would be "overkill".

JANITORIAL SERVICE AGREEMENT

MASTER BUILDING MAINTENANCE
POST OFFICE BOX 1087
VALLEY CENTER, CALIFORNIA 92082
(619) 749-2380

PROPOSAL SUBMITTED TO			DATE
Valley National Bank			April 10, 1989

ADDRESS
1001 First Avenue

CITY	STATE	ZIP
Valley Center	CA	92082

ATTENTION	PHONE
Mr. John Smith	(619) 749-0000

We propose to provide the following janitorial services:

DAILY SERVICE — five days per week

Thoroughly vacuum all carpeted areas.
Empty trash containers and replace liners.
Empty and clean ashtrays.
Dust desks, teller counters and all office furniture.
Spot clean entry door glass and office partition glass.
Remove ink marks and smudges from teller and lobby counters.
Clean lunchroom tables, counters and coffee area.
Thoroughly clean and sanitize restrooms.
Restock restroom supplies.
Spot clean carpeting as required.

WEEKLY SERVICE — one day per week

Perform all high and low dusting (i.e. window frames, chair legs,
    door mouldings, ceiling vents, etc.)
Spot clean door frames, walls and woodwork.

MONTHLY SERVICE — one day per month

Wash all windows, inside and out.

(Read Reverse Side)

We Hereby Propose and agree to provide janitorial service, equipment and supplies, complete in accordance with the above specifications, and subject to the terms and conditions found on both sides of this agreement, for the sum of:

THREE HUNDRED FIFTY AND 00/100   dollars ($ 350.00) per month.

Other terms:

Acceptance of Proposal The prices, specifications and terms outlined above and on the reverse are satisfactory and are hereby accepted. You are authorized to do the work as specified. Payment will be made as outlined above.

This agreement shall take effect as of _____ March 1 ___, 19 89 .

Owner_____ Contractor _Frederick R Massy_

© 1989 MBM • Box 1087, Valley Center, CA 92082 • (619) 749-2380 • Form # 101

SAMPLE ONE PAGE BID FORM (Front)

81

TERMS & CONDITIONS

SERVICES: The Owner hereby agrees to engage the services of the Contractor to furnish the janitorial and related services herein set forth and the Contractor agrees to perform such services to acceptable professional standards and for the compensation herein set forth. The Contractor may perform the services by any reasonable means and shall not be responsible for delays in performance caused by strike, lockout, act of God, accident, or any other circumstances beyond the Contractor's control.

EQUIPMENT AND SUPPLIES: The Contractor shall furnish all cleaning supplies and equipment necessary to perform the herein specified work. This does not include light bulbs and restroom supplies such as paper towels, hand soap, toilet paper, toilet seat covers, deodorants, etc. If the Owner so requests, these supplies can be furnished on a bill-back basis.

PAYMENT: Payment shall be due on the last day of each month in which services are performed. A late charge of one and one half (1½) percent per month (18% annual percentage rate) shall be paid by the Owner to the Contractor on any past due payment not received within ten (10) days after the last day of the month in which services are performed. If the account is referred to an agency or attorney for collection, all costs shall be at the expense of the Owner.

RIGHT TO TERMINATE: Notwithstanding any other section or provision of this Agreement, either party may terminate this Agreement upon thirty (30) days' written notice to the other party's representative at its respective address.

CHANGE IN WORK PERFORMED: The above price is based upon the areas to be serviced and the frequency of service outlined in the specifications. If there are changes in area or services, the Owner agrees to negotiate a reasonable price adjustment with the Contractor.

MODIFICATION: The parties may from time to time request changes in this agreement. Such changes, including any increase or decrease in the amount of the Contractor's compensation which are mutually agreed upon by and between the Owner and the Contractor, shall be effective when incorporated in written amendments to this agreement.

INSURANCE: The Contractor shall maintain liability and property damage insurance in form acceptable to the Owner, in full force and effect, throughout the term of this Agreement. The Contractor shall furnish to the Owner upon request a Certificate of Insurance evidencing such coverage.

INDEPENDENT CONTRACTOR: The parties intend that the Contractor in performing services herein specified shall act as an independent contractor and shall have control of the work and the manner in which it is performed. The Contractor shall select its own employees or agents and such employees and agents shall be responsible to the Contractor.

CONTRACTOR'S EMPLOYEES: It shall be understood and agreed that during the term of this agreement and for a period of three (3) months thereafter the Owner will not directly or indirectly hire any employee of the Contractor.

HOLIDAYS: The Contractor is not obligated to perform services on the following statutory holidays: New Year's Day, Washington's Birthday, Memorial Day, Independence Day, Labor Day, Veterans Day, Thanksgiving Day and Christmas Day. Services on holidays when requested by the Owner shall be performed at twice the normal daily rate.

APPLICABLE LAW: This agreement shall be governed by the laws of the State in which the services are performed. If any provision in this contract is held by any court to be invalid, void or unenforceable, the remaining provisions shall nevertheless continue in full force.

ENTIRE AGREEMENT: This agreement contains the entire agreement between the parties. All prior negotiations between the parties are merged in this agreement, and there are no understandings or agreements other than those incorporated herein. This agreement may not be modified except by written instrument signed by both parties.

SAMPLE ONE PAGE BID FORM (Back)

A one page form allows you to quickly prepare a professional-looking bid that covers all the basic information. Space is provided to write or type in the account name and address, date, cleaning specifications, price, terms and conditions. There is also a signature line for the customer's acceptance.

You can fill out the form at the job site and hand it to the customer for on-the-spot approval. Or you can type it up at your office and mail or hand-deliver it. By making a carbon copy of each form you fill out, you can keep an exact record in your files of all bids you give. This form may also be adapted to more complex or larger jobs by attaching a detailed specifications sheet. This is done by indicating "See Attached Specifications" on the front of the form.

One page bid forms are available through the publisher. See page 221 for further information.

THE CUSTOM PROPOSAL FORMAT

One of the most flexible and effective methods of preparing a proposal is to type it out on your company's letterhead stationery. (See sample, pages 86 to 89) This lets you customize your offer to exactly suit the needs of your client.

Your proposal can be as long or as short as the situation calls for. At a minimum, a typed letterhead proposal should include the following information:

1. The date.

2. The name and address of the client, plus the name of the individual in charge of receiving the bids, if you know it. (For example: Attn: Mr. Arthur Williams, Operations Manager)

3. Salutation ("Dear Mr. Williams", "Gentlemen", etc.)

4. An introductory sentence or two which states your intention. ("We hereby propose to...")

5. A list of the cleaning specifications (the exact cleaning tasks requested by the client). Cleaning specs may be arranged by frequency (daily, weekly, monthly, etc.); by specific areas (offices, lunchroom, warehouse, etc.); or by task (general cleaning, floor maintenance, restroom cleaning, etc.) Individual tasks should be spelled out in detail.

6. Equipment and supplies — As the contractor you will usually provide all of the cleaning equipment and supplies. But it needs to be spelled out who will provide and pay for restroom supplies, light bulbs, etc.

7. Insurance and bonding — At some point in your proposal, information on the type and amount of insurance you carry should be provided.

8. The terms and conditions — This includes your price, terms of payment, effective date of the contract, termination clause and any other terms or conditions you (or the owner) want to make a part of the agreement

9. Acceptance section — A place for the signatures of both parties. Once signed, the proposal becomes a legal binding contract.

OPTIONAL ENCLOSURES

You should apply your own creativity and package your bid in a way that sets it apart from all the others. Depending on the size and importance of the account, you may want to expand your proposal to include some or all of the following:

Customer references — Good customer references are a strong selling tool. They prove that you are a responsible company capable of fulfilling contract requirements to the customer's satisfaction. A good referral can make a difference in competitive bidding situations. You should include references whenever possible.

Some companies even include letters of reference from satisfied customers with their proposal. If they are well written these can be very impressive. If you have some particularly satisfied clients, you may want to ask if they would be willing to write such a letter for you.

Don't list any customer references you aren't sure of. Leave them out. It is also a good idea to have someone call and check on your references now and then.

Promotional material — You should include any promotional material that will enhance your company image, such as:

1. Your sales brochure.
2. Your company history.
3. Your quality control system.
4. A description of your training program, supervision and follow-up methods.
5. A brief resume of yourself and your managers and supervisors.
6. Any other creative promotional ideas you can think of that might sway the client in your favor.

Certificate Of Insurance — From the client's point of view, proof of liability insurance and bonding may be one of the most important considerations in hiring a cleaning contractor. In a long proposal you may want to highlight your insurance coverage by giving it a separate page or section in your proposal. You can obtain a "Certificate Of Insurance" from your insurance agent and show this in your proposal.

Table of contents — If you are putting together a lengthy proposal with a number of enclosures, you should include a table of contents. This allows the client to quickly find the exact information he is looking for, especially when comparing different aspects of several bids.

On a longer proposal it may also be helpful to use dividers between each section. The table of contents, if used, should go right after the cover letter.

CREATING AN ATTRACTIVE PROPOSAL

A proposal is much more than a piece of paper specifying certain cleaning duties and a price. A well-drafted proposal serves as an effective advertisement in itself. It is the culmination of all your promotion and as such, deserves your best effort. The appearance of the proposal must create a positive impression with the client. It could be the deciding factor in awarding the job.

Make it look sharp — no typing or spelling errors. Center the copy on the page, keeping the right and left margins as equal as possible, like a picture frame. If you don't type, hire a typist or secretarial service.

Word processing is a computer application that some contractors use to generate their proposals. Any personal computer with a word processing program and a letter quality printer can produce a completely customized proposal, perfectly typed, in a fraction of the time it would take to type and re-type on an ordinary typewriter.

Once you have your basic proposal format stored in computer memory, all you need to do is bring it up on the monitor, make a few changes to the specifications and personalize the cover letter. Then push a few keys and the computer will print out a crisp, clean proposal.

MASTER

BUILDING MAINTENANCE

P.O. BOX 1087 • VALLEY CENTER, CA 92082

(619) 749-2380

May 10, 1989

The Parkway Building
1010 Business Street
Valley Center, CA 92082

Attn: Mr. John Smith
       Manager

Dear Mr. Smith:

   We hereby propose and agree to perform the following janitorial services at the Parkway Building located at 1010 Business Street.

JANITORIAL SERVICES

DAILY SERVICE - 5 days per week

   Collect and remove all trash from the building.
   Replace plastic waste basket liners as necessary.
   Empty and clean all ashtrays.
   Vacuum all carpeting in offices and reception area.
   Dust desks, chairs and all other office furniture.
   Dust window sills, ledges and other flat surfaces.
   Spot clean water cooler.
   Spot clean doors, door frames and light switches.
   Spot clean glass entry doors.
   Wipe clean lunchroom tables, counters and chairs.
   Sweep and mop lunchroom.
   Spot clean plastic runners under desks.

WEEKLY SERVICE

   Spot clean carpeting.
   Damp mop plastic runners under desks.
   Machine buff lunchroom floor, refinish as necessary.
   Perform high and low dusting in offices (baseboards,
      chair and table legs, window and door mouldings, etc.)
   Hose off exterior stairway and courtyard.

MONTHLY SERVICE

   Dust all venetian blinds.
   Brush down wall and ceiling vents.

RESTROOM SERVICE - 5 days per week

Restock supplies (toilet paper, seat covers, paper towels
   and hand soap).
Empty trash containers.
Sweep and mop floor using disinfectant detergent.
Spot clean walls and partitions.
Clean all commodes and urinals.
Clean sinks and polish metal fixtures.
Polish mirrors.
Dust flat surfaces.

WINDOW CLEANING SERVICE

Clean all windows inside and out once every other month.
Clean office partition glass quarterly.

FLOOR CARE

Machine scrub, or strip and refinish tile floors in
   lunchroom and restrooms once every six months.

OTHER SERVICES

Replace light bulbs as required throughout building.
Carpet cleaning as requested will be performed at the
   price of 10¢ per square foot, with a minimum charge
   of $45 per cleaning.

EQUIPMENT AND SUPPLIES

We agree to provide all janitorial equipment and supplies
required to perform the above specified work. This does not
include light bulbs and restroom supplies (toilet paper, paper
towels, hand soap, deodorants, etc.) which we shall furnish
and bill for separately.

INSURANCE AND BONDING

We carry Comprehensive Liability Insurance in the amount
of $300,000.00 bodily injury, each person, $300,000.00 each
occurrence and $50,000.00 property damage. For your protec-
tion and ours we also carry a Janitorial Fidelity Bond.

PRICE

We agree to perform the above outlined services for the
sum of NINE HUNDRED AND TEN DOLLARS AND TWENTY-FIVE CENTS
($910.25) per month.

Our rate includes all costs for labor, materials, equipment, supervision, taxes and insurance required to fulfill
the cleaning specifications as outlined in this proposal.

TERMS AND CONDITIONS

PAYMENT

Payment shall be due on the last day of each month in which services are performed. A late charge of 1½ percent per month (18% annual percentage rate) shall be paid by the Owner to the Contractor on any past due payment not received within ten (10) days after the last day of the month in which services are performed. If the account is referred to an agency or attorney for collection, all costs shall be at the expense of the Owner.

RIGHT TO TERMINATE

Either party may terminate this agreement upon thirty (30) days' written notice.

CHANGE IN WORK PERFORMED

The above price is based upon the areas to be serviced and the frequency of service outlined in the specifications. If there are changes in area or services, the Owner agrees to negotiate a reasonable price adjustment with the Contractor.

MODIFICATION

The parties may from time to time request changes in this agreement. Such changes, including any increase or decrease in the amount of the Contractor's compensation which are mutually agreed upon by and between the Owner and the Contractor, shall be effective when incorporated in written amendments to this agreement.

INDEPENDENT CONTRACTOR

The parties intend that the Contractor in performing services herein specified shall act as an independent contractor and shall have control of the work and the manner in which it is performed. The Contractor shall select its own employees or agents and such employees and agents shall be responsible to the Contractor.

CONTRACTOR'S EMPLOYEES

It shall be understood and agreed that during the term of this agreement and for a period of three (3) months thereafter the Owner will not directly or indirectly hire any employee of the Contractor.

HOLIDAYS

The Contractor is not obligated to perform services on the following statutory holidays: New Year's Day, Washington's Birthday, Memorial Day, Labor Day, Independence Day, Thanksgiving Day, Christmas Day and Veterans Day. Services on holidays when requested by the Owner shall be performed at twice the normal daily rate.

APPLICABLE LAW

This agreement shall be governed by the laws of the State of California. If any provision in this contract is held by any court to be invalid, void or unenforceable, the remaining provisions shall nevertheless continue in full force.

ENTIRE AGREEMENT

This agreement contains the entire agreement between the parties. All prior negotiations between the parties are merged in this agreement, and there are no understandings or agreements other than those incorporated herein. This agreement may not be modified except by written instrument signed by both parties.

ACCEPTANCE

The above specifications, price, terms and conditions are satisfactory and are hereby accepted. This agreement shall take effect as of _____, 1989.

THE PARKWAY BUILDING   MASTER BUILDING MAINTENANCE

By_____   By___*Frederick R Massey*_____
        John Smith   Frederick R. Massey

_____
    Date of Acceptance

THE COVER LETTER

It is common practice to include a cover letter with your proposal to introduce it to the prospective client. (See sample, next page) The cover letter should be brief and should contain the following information:

1. An introduction to the proposal.
2. A few lines of promotion for your company — the quality of your service, etc.
3. A statement that if there are any questions, they should not hesitate to call.
4. A thank you to the client for the opportunity to submit the bid.
5. A personal signature.
6. Enclose your business card.

PRESENTING YOUR PROPOSAL

Whenever possible, arrange to **submit your proposal personally.** This way you know the bid is in the right hands. A hand-carried delivery shows your interest in the job and helps to establish a positive image for your company.

Occasionally, if the customer has the time, he may want to open and review your proposal on the spot. This will give you an opportunity to discuss your bid. If the customer says the proposal looks good but the price is more than he wanted to pay, you should be ready with suggestions as to how the cleaning specifications could be modified to allow you to lower your bid price.

Be sure you have a clear idea of what your profit margin is before you do any negotiating. You will usually have some price flexibility and everything is negotiable, but it must be done with tact. To say, "Well, maybe we can come down a little on our price," is unprofessional. The client will wonder just how you arrived at this "price".

Rather, any decrease in your bid should be tied to some reduction in cleaning requirements, no matter how slight. Be sure to let the client know that your rate reflects the **quality** of the service you intend to provide.

It some cases it will be necessary to **submit your bid by mail.** Send it by first class mail to the attention of the person who will be making the hiring decision. If the proposal is extremely important, you may wish to send it via the more expensive certified mail. That way you will get a signed receipt back in a few days, and both the client and the post office will be less likely to misplace your bid.

MASTER

BUILDING MAINTENANCE

P.O. BOX 1087 • VALLEY CENTER, CA 92082

(619) 749-2380

May 10, 1989

The Parkway Building
1010 Business Street
Valley Center, CA 92082

Attn: Mr. John Smith
        Manager

Dear Mr. Smith:

It was a pleasure meeting with you last Thursday, May 4. Thank you for the time you spent showing me your building.

Enclosed are two copies of our proposal to provide janitorial service for the Parkway Building. We are pleased to offer you a bid which is based on top-quality maintenance service at a competitive price.

If you have any questions about our proposed services, or if you need clarification on any point, please don't hestitate to call us. We appreciate the opportunity to submit this proposal and look forward to hearing from you soon.

Sincerely,

Frederick R. Massey
Owner

FRM:rm
Enclosures: (2)

SAMPLE COVER LETTER

Make three copies of the proposal. Sign two copies and send them to the client. Keep the third one for your records. When your bid is accepted the client should sign and return one copy and keep the other for his records.

After your bid is in, don't just sit back and wait, hoping for the client to call. After a few days call to see if your bid has been received. Be sure to mention that you will be glad to answer any questions or discuss the proposal further, either in person or over the phone. If you don't hear anything after another few days, call again to see if a decision has been reached. Don't heckle the client, but don't let him forget you either. Take every opportunity to impress him with your interest.

WHEN YOUR BID IS ACCEPTED

When your bid is accepted, show good business manners by calling, or writing a letter expressing your thanks. Once your bid has been approved, the real work begins. The most important priority now is to make a good first impression — this can carry you a long way.

If possible do the work yourself in the beginning, or assign an experienced employee to the job. Avoid training new employees on a brand new account. Most customers don't appreciate their building being used for training. Just about the time you get the employee properly trained and working efficiently, the account will be getting ready to drop you! By the same token it is usually bad business to assign a subcontractor immediately to a new account.

WHEN YOUR BID IS NOT ACCEPTED

You put a lot of effort into a bid and work it down to the best price you can offer. If it is an account you really want, you might knock off a few dollars just for good measure. You submit your bid and a few days later you get a phone call: "Thank you for considering our maintenance needs. We have decided to go with XYZ Company, as they have offered to do the work at a significantly lower rate."

Now that's discouraging. You know the account has been drastically underbid. You want to say: "Listen, there's no way that XYZ can provide the service you need at a price like that. When they fall on their face, give us a call. We'll do the job right, at a decent rate."

This may be true, but don't insult the customer by telling him he's made a mistake. Find a way to convey the same information **tactfully**! Write a short letter expressing your appreciation for being considered in the bidding. Mention that your bid was based on high quality service and still stands. You would like to be considered in any future bidding. Don't be surprised if you get a call in a few months — "Are you still interested? How soon can you start?"

WHEN YOU HAVE UNDERBID

Once you have been awarded a bid, it won't take long to realize if you have estimated correctly or not. If the bid is too low, you'll soon find yourself between a rock and a hard spot. Then what do you do? Cut back on service and risk losing the account, or ask for an increase and risk losing the account anyway? Or stick with the status quo and lose money?

Many contractors go with the first option. They lower the quality and try to squeeze by. They may get by for some time, but their business will suffer in the long run. Taking a loss is out of the question, so you are left with asking for an increase in price. If you are doing a good job you will probably get it. If you can't get a raise, then you will have to gracefully bow out and look for more profitable accounts.

HOW TO REQUEST A CONTRACT INCREASE

Over a period of time, a profitable account may gradually become unprofitable. This happens through the ordinary process of inflation, or through a more subtle process of gradually increasing specifications.

As time goes by, the janitor is asked to do this and that little extra chore — pick up around the entrance, water the plants, etc. These "little" chores, once performed, tend to become a part of the job and are quickly taken for granted by the customer. Taken one at a time they are too little to charge for, without feeling like you're nickel and diming the customer. But when you add them up, these little tasks can increase the overall job time considerably.

Many contractors are afraid to ask for a raise because they think that the customer will take the opportunity to put the job up for bid. But you shouldn't hesitate to ask for a contract increase when one is in order. Remember, your customers are used to receiving requests for increases from all their vendors, as well as giving regular raises to their employees.

Usually it is best to first raise the subject verbally, then confirm the increase with a letter. (See sample on the next page) This allows for some negotiation and gives you a chance to better explain the reasons for your request for a contract increase. If the client is satisfied with your service, chances are good that you will be able to get your raise. In any event, if the account has become marginal or unprofitable, you have little or nothing to lose. Remember, a contract increase is as good as a new account and easier to sell.

MASTER

BUILDING MAINTENANCE

P.O. BOX 1087 • VALLEY CENTER, CA 92082

(619) 749-2380

March 10, 1989

Midway Office Building, Inc.
12921 Palm Avenue
Valley Center, CA 92082

Attn: Mr. Ellis R. Parker
       Manager

Dear Mr. Parker:

   This letter is to confirm our discussion of yesterday
regarding the increase in our monthly cleaning rate to
$575.00 per month, effective April 1, 1989. All other
terms of our maintenance agreement remain unchanged and
in full effect.

   Please indicate your agreement and approval by signing
and returning the original copy of this letter to our office.
The second copy is for your records.

   Your continued patronage is greatly appreciated. Many
thanks.

                              Sincerely,

                              Frederick R. Massey

                              Frederick R. Massey
                              Owner

APPROVED:

MIDWAY OFFICE BUILDING, INC.

_____

By Ellis R. Parker

_____

Date

SAMPLE CONTRACT INCREASE LETTER

Chapter 6
MANAGING YOUR BUSINESS

Once you've got the accounts, how do you keep them? There are no big secrets — you've just got to be able to back up your words with work. If you are not able to get the job done there is no trick that will save you. But you can help yourself tremendously by careful planning and organization.

STARTING A NEW ACCOUNT

When you start a new account, make sure you are familiar with the operational aspects of the building. If you haven't made notes of this during your building survey, you should arrange to go to the account prior to your first work day and obtain the information. This will save you much time and frustration later on. Here are some key things to find out about:

Who to contact — There is usually one person at the account who is assigned the responsibility for the building maintenance. This is the person you will be dealing with in servicing the account.

Alarm systems — Location of controls, how to turn them off and reset them, if need be.

Emergency procedures — Know the location of circuit breakers, fuse boxes and the main water shutoff.

Storage rooms — Know where the janitor rooms or storage closets are located.

Trash disposal — Location of dumpsters and any special procedures that need to be followed. For instance, banks often require that the teller trash be saved for several days before being thrown out.

Location of light switches — Hunting for light switches in the dark at a new account is no fun. Even if you know where all the switches are, it is a good idea to always carry a small pocket flashlight for emergencies. Also find out which lights are to be left on and which are to be turned off.

Building keys — Make sure the key you have been given actually opens the door. Try it out first. Often the manager will have a duplicate key made for you, and sometimes it doesn't work. (Not to mention when he gives you the wrong key!) Also determine if you are going to need additional keys for storerooms and offices. Special skeleton keys for opening restroom supply dispensers are available from janitorial suppliers.

As your business grows, you will accumulate keys by the pound. For security reasons, never put an account name on a key. Instead, code each key with a letter or number. The locksmith shop can stamp the keys for you or you can use tape or a label maker. Keep a duplicate of each key at your office.

EQUIPMENT STORAGE

Another important consideration when you are starting a new account is storage of equipment and supplies. Which supplies will be stored at the work site and which will remain in your vehicle? If you are doing route work the expensive equipment (floor machines, vacuums, etc.) can be transported by you or your employees from one site to the next. This eliminates buying extra equipment for each new account, keeping equipment expense to a minimum. It may be helpful to store some of your cleaning supplies at each location, if a closet is provided. But be sure that the employees of the business you service aren't helping themselves.

SCHEDULING PERIODIC OR PROJECT CLEANING

Most accounts you service will require the performance of periodic or "project" cleaning tasks. Periodic cleaning duties are those non-daily specifications in your contract that must be performed monthly, bi-monthly, semi-annually, etc., such as floor stripping or carpet cleaning.

There is an almost universal tendency in this business to neglect these infrequent duties. This is a major cause of customer dissatisfaction and lost accounts. To avoid this you need to set up a system for keeping track of, and handling, project work. One way to keep track of the periodic duties for your accounts is to list them by date on a large wall calendar. This will allow you to see at a glance when periodic cleaning duties come due.

Large cleaning companies which have the necessary manpower employ specialized teams of window cleaners and floor care people (waxers) to travel from account to account handling project work. But if you are a smaller company you won't have this luxury. In the beginning you will have to do the project work yourself, or schedule one of your employees who wants extra work. You can also look into hiring temporary workers to help you on large, infrequent jobs. (Just make sure you supervise them closely!)

Some types of periodic cleaning such as high/low dusting or detail vacuuming can be incorporated into the regular cleaning routine. (See pages 135 and 136) Another option is to subcontract your project work. For instance, you could have a window cleaning company take care of your high windows, and a carpet cleaner with specialized equipment handle your carpet cleaning.

BE SELECTIVE

When you advertise yourself as a cleaning contractor you will get calls for all sorts of unusual jobs (like cleaning up after a fire in a meat packing plant). There are many cleaning related jobs that you might be able to take on and even make money at, but you just don't want them. Some jobs are too small, others are too large and some will just tie up too much of your time and energy. When you get a call for a job you really don't want, just politely decline. Be selective and do what's best for your business.

Seven day per week accounts — Accounts that are open seven days per week put extra pressure on a maintenance company. The work must be done every day so there are no days off to "regroup". These jobs tend to beat you down and limit the growth of your company.

Practically speaking, to maintain seven day accounts for any length of time requires two separate crews. This costs you extra time and money in terms of scheduling, training and supervision. Also many seven day per week accounts work straight through the ordinary holidays. This can cause scheduling headaches and employee dissatisfaction, even when you have two crews.

Twenty-four hour accounts — Accounts that are open 24 hours require you to work around the public or the employees in the building. This inevitably causes work slowdown and safety hazards. You cannot expect to achieve the same production rates that you can in an empty building. Twenty-four hour accounts also require a different attitude toward cleaning, since your work is usually messed up as quickly as it is done.

Another problem with the seven day per week, 24 hour accounts is that they tend to turn over managers quickly. And unfortunately new managers often make changes in staff and services. This can cause you to lose the account in spite of your best efforts.

Even with these difficulties there is money to be made in servicing these accounts. But it takes good organization and strong, flexible crews and supervisors. The important thing is to know what you are getting into before you bid on this type of work. You want to set a price that will make the extra effort worth your while.

CUSTOMER RECORDS

Accurate customer records are essential. Commercial accounts will require an 8½" x 11" file folder each. All information, starting with the initial phone message, should be included in this file — a copy of the proposal, work specifications, copies of correspondence, estimating work sheets, a record of equipment and supplies stored at the account, etc. Paperwork on any terminated account should be separated into an "inactive file", not thrown away. You never know when the information can be of use again.

Most residential and one-time jobs can be kept track of easily on 3x5 or 4x6 cards. These can be arranged alphabetically, by last name, in a card file (a plastic recipe box will do to start). On completing each job, fill out a card for the customer. It should include:

1. Name, address and phone number.
2. A description of the work done, by whom and the time it took to complete.
3. Date the work was done.
4. Price.
5. Note how the customer heard of you.
6. Directions, if difficult to find.
7. Notes on the job — this information is important! Each job will have its idiosyncrasies and it is a good idea for you or your crew to be prepared for them (for example, "mean dog").

Day, Mary				749-0000
142 Hilldale Blvd.				
Any Town				How: Yellow Pages
DATE	PRICE	TIME	JOB	NOTES
11/17/88	$40	2½ hr.	Window cleaning	Heavy smoke film inside
3/15/89	$48	2¾ hr.	Window cleaning	Includes screens
4/10/89	$125	3 hr.	Strip + re-wax entry and dining room floor	

RESIDENTIAL BILLING

It is usually not necessary to prepare an invoice for small one-time jobs such as window cleaning. The customer's cancelled check serves as their receipt. Occasionally a customer may request a receipt, so you should carry a few invoices or a cash receipts book in your glove compartment.

For larger residential jobs, such as carpet and upholstery cleaning, it is a good idea to get a signed work order before starting the job. You can buy standard forms at a stationery store.

One of the advantages of residential cleaning is that you get paid on the spot. If you are doing regularly scheduled work for homeowners, such as housecleaning, it may be a good selling point to bill for your services on a monthly basis. But it is not usually a good idea to extend credit on one-time jobs. By the time the customer gets around to paying your bill the floors or windows are dirty again, and she may decide to simply put off or ignore your billing. Then you have a collection problem.

COMMERCIAL BILLING

Commercial customers are normally billed toward the end of the month in which the work is performed. You can use standard invoice forms (available at stationery stores) and just type or stamp your company name in. For a more professional-looking invoice, have your company name and address printed in. (See sample, next page) The cost is nominal.

Statement forms (invoices) come with a carbon copy which you should keep as your record. They are normally perforated so the customer can return the upper portion of the bill with his payment. The bill will include your regular monthly rate, as well as any extra work you have done which the customer has already agreed to pay for.

Occasionally, it may be necessary to provide a credit for work not done or improperly done. This should also be indicated on the bill. The cost of supplies you have purchased for the account, over and above what is covered in the contract, should also be included. (See "Marking Up Supplies" on page 101.)

Some accounts pay very slowly. You may not have received the money from the previous month's bill when it comes time to prepare the next month's billing. Enter the former amount due as a "Balance Forward" and add it into the total amount due. (See "Cash Flow" later in this chapter.)

STATEMENT

MASTER BUILDING MAINTENANCE
POST OFFICE BOX 1087
VALLEY CENTER, CALIFORNIA 92082
(619) 749-2380

AMOUNT ENCLOSED $_____

DATE	TERMS
March 20,1989	

Valley National Bank

1001 First Avenue

Valley Center, CA   92082

PAY LAST BALANCE
IN THIS COLUMN

PLEASE DETACH AND RETURN WITH YOUR REMITTANCE

DATE AND DESCRIPTION	CHARGES	CREDITS	
	PREVIOUS BALANCE →		
Janitorial service for March 1989	$750.00		
Supplies:			
1 case hand towels	25.00		
½ case kitchen towels	12.50		
2 8' neon bulbs	14.00		$801.50

MASTER BUILDING MAINTENANCE

Thank You

SAMPLE INVOICE

MARKING UP SUPPLIES

Restroom supplies (paper towels, toilet tissue, hand soap, etc.), which you supply to the client and bill for separately, should be marked up at least enough to cover all your costs in providing the products. This includes purchasing, stocking and monitoring.

The customer is receiving a **delivered product** and should expect to pay a little extra for this service. If you provide these supplies at cost, your time and expense of doing so is taken for granted and you are losing money as well.

In cases where it is not practical to mark up the supplies directly, you can estimate the usage and work in an allowance for this in your bid. A minimum mark-up would be 10% to 15% of the cost of the supplies. Even a mark-up of 50% would not be unreasonable when you consider all the costs, including your time.

CASH FLOW

In contract cleaning there is always a time lag between the performance of the work and receipt of the money. Some accounts will stretch this time up to 60 days or more. During a recession this lag gets longer and longer. What is happening? The slow-paying customers are using "your money" (the money in their budget intended for you) while they put your invoice on the bottom of the pile.

Slow payers are murder in this business. When they delay payment to you, it makes it hard for you to meet your payroll and other expenses on time.

When a customer's account becomes past due you should get in touch with them immediately. Don't let them slide along for weeks or months assuming they will pay eventually. If they aren't paying you, then chances are they aren't paying their other services and suppliers. Maybe they are getting ready to declare bankruptcy, or take a permanent vacation in Mexico! Keep on top of the situation and protect yourself.

To find out what is going on, call and inquire — have they received your invoice or perhaps overlooked it? It is helpful if you can get on a first name basis with the customer's bookkeeper. It is much harder for them to put off a real person than it is to dismiss a company name on a piece of paper.

There are several things you can do to encourage customers to pay promptly. You might consider offering a 1% to 2% discount if the bill is paid within ten days of the due date. Or you can specify a penalty of 1½% interest per month on bills that are past due. These conditions should all be included in your contract, and agreed to in advance by the customer, so there are no misunderstandings.

Whenever possible, bill on the 20th of the month with payment due at the end of the month, and past due by the 10th of the following month. This will help your cash flow considerably.

CONTROLLING YOUR COSTS

Your goal in professional cleaning is to first **make money** and spend it only when in some way it helps you to make more money. If you are a small company, one of the big competitive advantages you have is low overhead. So look for ways to save money and keep your overhead expenses to an absolute minimum.

There is always the temptation when starting a new venture to overspend, trying to create an impression of big business and success. Don't waste your money. If you give your customers good quality service they will be far more impressed.

When you are in business for yourself, everyone will try to sell you more than you need. Printers, banks, the telephone company and all your suppliers will suggest all sorts of expensive options and gadgets. You can't blame them — that's their business, making money off you. The age-old rule of thumb is *never take advice from someone who is trying to sell you something.*

TIPS ON CUSTOMER RELATIONS

To really succeed the owner of a janitorial company must develop a **solution-oriented attitude.** This means facing problems in a businesslike and unemotional way, looking for ways to solve problems, rather than becoming defensive or seeking escape routes.

Check with your customers on a regular basis to make sure everything is going smoothly. When problems do come up, you can discuss them and come to an understanding or, if necessary, a compromise. Sometimes you aren't doing what was agreed upon, and sometimes they will be trying to stretch the agreement to include some extra work. As long as you communicate you will be able to prevent minor irritations from escalating into major problems.

A common mistake made by maintenance contractors is to avoid the account manager. They shy away from him, fearing an unpleasant confrontation and complaints. They imagine if they don't confront the problems they will go away. This is one of the main causes of the high turnover in janitorial accounts. The contractor and the customer avoid communicating with one another until the final communication — a termination notice in the mail!

HANDLING COMPLAINTS

Who knows how it got started, but the accepted standard procedure for lodging a complaint seems to be to leave a note in a conspicuous place where the janitor can see it. You will find these little scraps of paper stuck on desks, the cleaning closet door, on the mirror above the bathroom sink or over a light switch. The accepted standard procedure that many janitors follow is to deposit these little notes directly in the trash. If the problem isn't taken care of the notes continue — each one getting a little more direct.

If someone takes the time to write a note, then they feel it is important. Whether or not the problem is legitimate, it should be dealt with right away. If it is a request for a service that is not included in the contract, then it needs to be discussed with the client. Don't disregard a note or misunderstandings will develop.

Complaints that are phoned in are much easier to deal with, because there is direct communication and the problem can be more quickly resolved. Urge all of your customers to contact you right away, over the phone, if they have any questions or problems. Be sure you return calls as soon as possible. When customers call with a problem and you don't get back to them, they really get irritated.

Sometimes it is a tenant who is complaining, someone who doesn't know what the maintenance contract calls for. They may be griping about some condition that isn't even a part of your agreement with the building owner. You need to take the initiative and bring the problem to the attention of the owner. That way, he or she can talk to the tenant and straighten things out, or change the contract if need be.

If you stress service and customer satisfaction first, you will have few complaints.

WHEN YOU LOSE AN ACCOUNT

Regardless of what reasons were given for your termination, it is good policy to write a letter thanking the customer for using your company — "for the opportunity of doing business with you". A polite letter ends the relationship on a positive note and keeps the door open in case things should change in the future.

If you were doing the job well, the chances are they didn't appreciate it — took it all for granted. After a few months of suffering along with some mediocre maintenance firm they may well change their attitude and want you back.

DON'T TAKE IT ALL TOO SERIOUSLY

No matter what size your company is you have to maintain an independent spirit. You can't afford to get bogged down in any one account and its problems. This requires the right attitude and a strong sense of self-respect. A sense of humor also comes in handy.

Take pride in your work, but don't become a slave to it. It is easy to get so busy working that you stop thinking and planning. Then you lose sight of your goal and the reason you started working in the first place. If you lose your perspective you become an employee again, a prisoner of your own business.

Remember, you are running the business. Don't let it run you. Why lose sleep over problems? Taking pride in your work and giving attention to detail are important, but if you are an unbending perfectionist, you may go crazy in this business.

It's a big game really. Do a good job and don't take it all too seriously. Then you can **enjoy** your business.

DIVERSIFICATION — PROFITABLE SIDELINES

When you do good work your customers will always be asking, "Can you do this?" or "Can you handle that?" There will be many opportunities to branch out into profitable sidelines.

Some services, like residential window cleaning, are easy to get into and don't require much capital investment. Other services, such as disaster restoration, require experience, training and a sizeable investment in specialized equipment. Generally speaking the more training and money you need to provide a special service, the less competition you will encounter. And the less competition there is, the more you can charge.

Before making the decision to branch out into a new field, you should consider both the potential market for the service and the start-up investment you will need to make. Here are a few questions to ask yourself: "Can I generate enough work to amortize the cost of the equipment and still make a profit? How much will it cost to promote the new service? How much time will I need to put into it?"

You should also consider whether or not the service fits in well with what you already do. For example, window cleaning, carpet cleaning and hard floor care are naturals for a janitorial company. Swimming pool maintenance is a little further afield. What you want are services you can sell to your existing customers to make additional profits on your accounts. Add-on sales are smart business! Here are some of the areas you can diversify into:

maid service	carpet cleaning
window cleaning	construction clean-up
wall and ceiling cleaning	pest extermination
landscaping and lawn care	asbestos removal
restroom sanitizing	hard floor care
disaster clean-up	snow removal
security or guard service	blind cleaning
parking lot sweeping	parking lot restriping
swimming pool maintenance	window tinting
chimney sweeping	drapery cleaning
interior plant service	upholstery cleaning
furniture cleaning	painting
handyman work	pressure washing
fluorescent light cleaning	metal cleaning
consulting	carpet dyeing
apartment and vacancy cleaning	model home cleaning
	janitorial supply sales

When making any decision to diversify, keep in mind that you can't do everything. There are only 24 hours in a day. Don't spread yourself too thin!

CONTROLLING YOUR BUSINESS GROWTH

With quality work and aggressive promotion, a janitorial business can be expanded rapidly. However, allowing your business to grow too quickly in an uncontrolled way can be detrimental to your long range success. It is not uncommon for a new contractor to quickly build up a large monthly volume, then six months later he is out of business.

It takes careful planning and organization to grow really big and still maintain quality service on each job you contract. There is a quality/quantity trade-off that is hard to balance in the professional cleaning business. Simply put, this means that the bigger your firm is, the more difficult it becomes to maintain quality work at the individual account level.

Most employees won't pay as much attention to detail as you do, and if you are busy concentrating on that next big account, who is minding the store? More precisely, who is making sure that the accounts are getting the personal attention and quality cleaning service they were promised?

The customer doesn't care how big your janitorial company is. He cares about one thing — getting his money's worth. If he sees that your cleaning company is not going to fulfill its promises, he will find someone else.

Some large cleaning contractors seem to have completely given up trying to hold the line on quality. They have become all-out quantity oriented. Their goal seems to be not so much to get good accounts and keep them, but rather to land more accounts in any given period of time than they lose. Doing business in this fashion is hard on the nerves.

It is up to you to decide what you want out of your business. Bigger is not always better. Many cleaning contractors choose to stop expanding at a point where they can still remain personally involved in the work — supervising employees, inspecting the accounts and communicating regularly with their customers. They could expand their businesses if they wanted to, but they feel more comfortable at a level where they can still keep an eye on everything.

SET A PACE YOU CAN MAINTAIN

When you are starting from scratch you are hustling for any job you can get. Problems begin when the business starts to roll in and you've still got that "hungry" attitude. If you continue to take on every job, you will find that you have such an overwhelming quantity of work that you don't have the time to do any one job well, not even time to properly train or supervise your employees.

Overextension (taking on more work than you can handle) is a common mistake made by beginners in the maintenance business. Don't let your initial enthusiasm eat you up. In order to build a business that will last, you've got to set a pace you can maintain.

It is much more satisfying to develop your business gradually and steadily, always considering quality as well as quantity of work.

Chapter 7
EXPANDING YOUR BUSINESS WITH EMPLOYEES

The beginner in the cleaning business generally starts out as a one-man operation. Sometimes he or she will enjoy the good fortune of having a spouse who is also enthusiastic about the new venture. One-man or husband-wife outfits have many advantages. As owner, you are right on top of everything and can be sure of maximum quality control. You can act fast and implement your ideas immediately. You do all your own selling, bidding and servicing. When you are out on the job involved in the work you are constantly learning, meeting people and discovering new ways to get more business.

As your business grows you can weed out less profitable accounts as better ones are secured, and eventually develop a concentrated route of quality accounts. With the right accounts you may be making $3,500 a month, possibly more. Still, there are only 24 hours in a day and you've got to sleep and eat, too. There is a limit to what one person can do. If you want to expand you are going to have to think in terms of hiring.

A SYSTEM FOR EXPANDING

1. In the beginning, do as much of the work as you can reasonably handle yourself, or with employees who work directly with you. This is practical because you keep payroll expense down as well as get plenty of actual cleaning experience. Your quality control is at a maximum.

2. Hire one employee at a time and train him or her to do the job the way you want it done. Work as a crew with one or two helpers. It makes the work go faster and they will learn to work efficiently.

3. As you acquire new accounts, always try to clean them yourself to establish that all-important good first impression. This is also the best way to determine exactly how long it takes to get the job done. Leave your trained employees on the established accounts.

4. Keep moving ahead, handling the new accounts yourself and regularly checking the work on the established accounts. Control your promotional efforts, not taking on more work than you can handle until you are geared up for it.

5. If you want to expand past the point where you can personally supervise the work, you will need to recruit a reliable working supervisor. This individual will take the workload off you, so you can concentrate on cultivating new accounts. Hire additional supervisors as you expand.

6. To build a really large organization you'll need to promote or hire an operations manager to handle the day-to-day operation of your company. You can then spend most of your time on the exciting marketing aspects of the business.

FINDING THE RIGHT EMPLOYEES

Your first step is to decide what kind of individuals will work out best for you. Beginners often think that an ideal set-up would be to hire a few full-time employees to take care of all the accounts. However, it is not easy to find motivated full-time maintenance employees who will stick around for long. Part-time employees often work out better.

Have you ever observed the day shift maintenance people in a large government building? Some of them appear to be moving in slow motion. It makes your eyes hurt to look at them! These people are bored stiff. Eight hours a day of routine cleaning is too much for most employees. They literally drag themselves from one coffee break to the next. There are individuals who can be positive and effective in these situations, but they are the exception.

Part-time employees are often highly motivated. Many of them are moonlighters who hold down a full-time job but need extra money. They will often be your very best workers — fast and efficient. Part-timers aren't interested in trying to look busy. They want to get the work done and go home. Because they only work a few hours a night, they don't get bored with the job.

Part-time employees usually have a good feeling about their work and themselves. Society says it's fine to work for a lower wage when it is part-time, on the side. Working full time at minimum wage is often viewed as a "can't get anything better" situation. Part-time workers can save you a good deal of money, too. They do not expect to receive as many benefits as full-time employees, and you won't have to pay overtime for other work they do which amounts to less than 40 hours per week.

Another benefit of hiring a number of part-timers as opposed to a few full-timers, is that you have a larger labor pool of workers to call on when new or special jobs pop up. Also, if one of your part-time staff quits suddenly, you are not left with as big a hole in your operation as when a full-timer drops out.

College students are often interested in working part-time. Some companies draw most of their workers from the local campus.

Handicapped employees have proven time and again that they can excel on any job if their particular handicap does not physically exclude them. They often have a lower rate of turnover and are responsible and punctual. In a field that depends so heavily on employee reliability, the handicapped should not be underestimated.

Couples are perfect for maintenance work. There is a natural desire among many couples to find work they can do together. Husband and wife teams appreciate the opportunity to work together and will tend to be conscientious in their work. By sharing the job, couples can work quickly and efficiently, handling a number of accounts each evening.

Friends and relations — New businessmen are often tempted to employ friends and relatives. This can cause real problems because of the familiarity that already exists. Some people will take advantage of your friendship — it is difficult to properly supervise a close acquaintance. If they are doing a lousy job, you are in the uncomfortable position of losing either your friend or your customer.

HELP WANTED ADS

Most people looking for janitorial work look in the Help Wanted section of the newspaper under "Janitors". This is where you should advertise. Your help wanted ads should be directed to the kind of individuals you want to hire. Your ads should define the job and the employee qualifications, so you don't attract a lot of applicants who aren't right for the job — a waste of your time and theirs.

If you are near a college, you can try the student newspaper or placement service.

TAKING APPLICATIONS

Usually a prospective employee will initially contact you over the phone. You'll find you can weed out many callers by briefly explaining the type of job opening you have — the hours, duties and starting pay. Then, if the job hunter expresses interest in the opening, have him or her come in and fill out an application. The more qualified applications you receive, the better your chance of finding the right employee. Employment application forms are available at any stationers.

You should use a form which is up-to-date and in compliance with Equal Opportunity Laws. Nowadays, questions concerning marital status, age, nationality, race, religion, sex, physical handicap, etc. are not allowed.

Applicants should be able to provide a local phone number and address where they can actually be reached. Hiring transients will seldom benefit your business. Each applicant should be able to provide a full employment history and references. If they can't remember where they have worked the last few years, you don't want them!

Although first time job hunters won't have employer references, they should have at least three personal character references. Be sure to let the applicant know that you **will** be checking their references. Ask that they provide telephone numbers of former employers to speed up the checking process. This will weed out the losers who list bogus references, just betting that you won't take the trouble to check. And the fact is that most employers do not check references. Don't make that mistake. One hasty hiring decision can undo a lot of your hard work.

Be sure your prospective employee signs the bottom of the application form. This authorizes you to verify the statements they have made in their application (i.e. to check their references). If the applicant refuses to sign, it should tell you something!

INTERVIEWING

When you meet the prospective employee you should have their application in front of you. Also have a note pad and pen and be ready to take notes. Be congenial and do your best to put the applicant at ease. (Remember how you felt the last time you applied for a job?) Keep your questions and the conversation relevant to the job at hand. Stay away from questions that violate Equal Opportunity and Anti-Discrimination laws.

As you review and discuss the applicant's previous employment, take note of how long the applicant stayed with each job and also how long they were out of work between jobs. You may want to inquire about any long periods of unemployment. Review each application carefully, but remember — in interviewing you will find that there is often more information revealed in the employee's eyes and behavior than there is on the paper.

Honesty is the single most critical factor in hiring janitorial employees. Your employees will be left alone in office buildings with unlimited access to all sorts of valuable equipment — plenty of opportunity to steal. Ask yourself, "Can

I trust this person with the keys?" If you have any doubts about the applicant's character, beware.

You have got to be a good judge of character when it comes to interviewing and hiring janitors. What you really want to look for is reliability, honesty and trustworthiness. Experience is an obvious asset, but you are better off with a reliable novice than an irresponsible "expert".

NOTE: Until recently many larger janitorial contractors relied on polygraph tests to screen out undesirable applicants. Now the Employee Polygraph Protection Act of 1988 has prohibited that practice for most private employers.

Take your time and be thorough. Check references, use good judgment and trust your own feelings. If a candidate looks good on paper but you just don't feel comfortable with him or her, keep looking. Remember, you are not obligated to hire the first person who walks in the door. You are looking for the **right** person, someone you can count on. So keep looking until you are satisfied you have found the right employee.

GETTING A NEW EMPLOYEE STARTED

Upon hiring, each employee should receive:

1. **A W-4 Form** — so you know how much tax to withhold from his or her wages. (See "Employee Records", page 120)

2. **A Form I-9** — to verify that the employee is legally eligible to work in the U.S. (See "Complying With The IRCA", page 120)

3. **An I.D. card** — for identification to the building manager on the accounts he or she will work.

4. **A copy of your company policies** — so your employee knows what is expected. It is important that these rules not be condescending in tone. They should provide guidelines, not threats.

5. **A copy of the work specifications** for the particular job(s) he or she will be doing. (See sample, next page) This should be a clear, easy-to-understand list of the cleaning requirements for the job. It should be prepared directly from the cleaning specifications in the proposal.

The work outline should include an exact description of the duties they are to perform. If there are periodic cleaning duties, it should indicate their frequencies (once a month, quarterly, etc.) It is especially important to include any peculiarities of the job, such as "Do not clean in the computer room".

MASTER

BUILDING MAINTENANCE

P.O. BOX 1087 • VALLEY CENTER, CA 92082

(619) 749-2380

EMPLOYEE WORK SPECIFICATIONS

Account: An Office Building

Location: Downtown

Frequency: Five days per week, Monday through Friday

Cleaning Time: After 5:30 p.m. Try to be done by 10 p.m.

CLEANING DUTIES

TRASH

- Dump ashtrays. Clean and shine them.
- Empty all waste baskets and replace liners when necessary.
- Dump trash in dumpster on west side of building.

DUSTING

- Daily: Dust all flat surfaces you can easily reach from
  a standing position, using treated dust cloths. This includes chairs, desks, file cabinets, window sills, ledges,
  telephones and office furniture.
- Once a week: Dust chair and table legs, tops of baseboards,
  window and door mouldings.
- Once a month: Dust all venetian blinds. There are twenty
  sets of blinds in the building, plus one in the reception
  room. Dust one set of blinds each night to satisfy this
  requirement.

GENERAL CLEANING

- Clean glass entry doors, using spray cleaner. Spot clean
  office desks and tables with all-purpose solution in
  trigger sprayer.
- Do not use all-purpose spray on wood desk in President's
  office (Suite A). Use dust cloth only.
- Remove all fingerprints from glass table in conference
  room each day using window cleaner in spray bottle and
  a dry cloth. Do not use treated dust cloths.
- As you work, watch for fingerprints and smudges around
  light switches and on doors and mouldings. Spot clean
  these areas and the water cooler each day.
- Wipe counters and tables in lunchroom with damp sponge
  kept under the sink.
- Do not clean the lockers, sink, cabinets or coffee machine.
  These are not our responsibility.

                                              (contd.)

Employee Work Specifications (contd.)

<u>FLOORS</u>

_   In the lunchroom, wipe tables clean, then sweep tile floor
    with the push broom.
-   Damp mop tile floors using neutral detergent (blue label).

<u>CARPETING</u>

-   Vacuum carpeting in all office areas. Be sure to go under
    all desks and tables.
-   Vacuum the plastic runners under the desks also. Spot
    clean the runners where needed and damp mop them once a
    week, more often if necessary.

<u>RESTROOMS</u>

-   Empty the restroom trash when you collect the lunchroom
    trash. Take note of what paper supplies you will need.
    Bring these supplies with you when you return to clean
    the restroom, to save an extra trip.
-   Refill the dispensers first.
-   Sweep out the restrooms when you do the lunchroom. Sweep
    <u>behind</u> the toilet bases and the trash can.
-   Spray clean toilets. Do a thorough job. Clean both sides
    of toilet seats and behind the seat where it connects to
    the tank. Also around the base of the toilets.
-   Use acid bowl cleaner once a week.
-   Spray clean sinks and mirrors. Wipe these surfaces dry,
    leaving no streaks or water spots. If sinks are espe-
    cially dirty, use the white nylon scrub pad. Be sure to
    rinse sink well, then wipe dry. Polish all metal hardware
    with dry cloth.
-   As you are cleaning, look for spots and smudges on walls
    and partitions. Spray and wipe clean.
-   Dust flat surfaces on the tops of paper towel dispensers
    and partitions daily. Once a week clean the ceiling
    vents.
-   Wet mop the floor with the disinfectant-detergent. Do
    not slop on baseboards and be sure not to leave any
    mop strings.

<u>NOTES</u>

-   Do <u>not</u> organize desks. Clean <u>around</u> paperwork.
-   Be very careful not to bang the vacuum cleaner against
    the antique desk in President's office (Suite A).
-   Do not go into the computer room. It is not our
    responsibility.
-   If you have problems or run into anything unusual, call
    the office right away at 749-2380.

Make three copies of the specifications — one for your customer file, one for the supervisor and one for the employee. Specs can also be posted in the janitor's room at the account. Any time there is a change in requirements, or something special pops up, you should enter it on the cleaning specs. Be sure to relay the information to the employee on the job!

WAGES

Traditionally, maintenance employees have been paid less than other more "skilled" positions. People are inclined to think that anyone can do cleaning work. While it is true that anyone can go through the motions of cleaning, very few are really good at it.

Going through the motions may be enough to get by when you are working for the government, but in private contracting you've got to have fast, efficient and motivated employees. You don't get paid just for showing up in this business. By offering a somewhat higher wage you will be able to attract top employees away from other businesses that are paying minimum wage.

Of course, it takes more than money to motivate some people. If you've got someone really good, give them as much responsibility as they want or can handle. See that they don't get that futile feeling of being trapped in a dead-end situation. If you are going to expand, you are going to need a working crew leader or supervisor. Let a good employee know this, so that he or she has something to work toward.

PAYING BY ACCOUNT

It is a common practice among cleaning contractors to pay by the account rather than by the hour. This encourages employees to work quickly and efficiently. Under this system a good maintenance worker will make considerably more per hour than the average hourly worker, without increasing your labor expense.

Here's how this works. When you get a new account, you first go in and work it yourself. This way you get the place in shape and make a good first impression. You also determine exactly what the job takes and how long it takes. Based on your own first-hand knowledge of the work, you can set a flat rate for this account. In setting a time standard, keep in mind that most employees will not work as fast as you do. You must be sure to set a realistic time to do the job. The rate must always provide at least the legal minimum hourly wage.

Example: If you determine the job will take an average employee three hours per night, you may set your flat rate at $15 per night. This equals a starting pay of $5 per hour. In the beginning, you will work with the employee and show him or her how to get the job done right in three hours.

For the first week or so, they may be pressed to do this. Let them know that it takes a while to learn the job and you will pay for whatever reasonable time they run over. If the employee is a good worker, he or she will soon be getting the work done in three hours. Then, after they become really familiar with the work and develop a good system, they may be able to complete the job satisfactorily in two and one half hours. Now they are making $6 per hour, while your labor cost holds constant.

MILEAGE ALLOWANCES

If employees are using their own vehicles to travel from one job site to the next, you could consider paying them a mileage allowance (15¢ to 20¢ a mile) or including travel time in their regular wage.

If you don't do this, a new employee probably won't kick about it at first. But after a while he starts to think about what it is costing him in time and money driving all over the countryside.

SUPERVISION

In the beginning, **you** will be the supervisor going from one account to the next, checking the work, keeping in touch with the employees and communicating with the account manager.

Later, when your business expands, you may appoint crew leaders, working supervisors and eventually full-time supervisors. No matter who is doing the supervising, the principles remain the same.

A BASIC ATTITUDE OF RESPECT — Your basic attitude toward your employees will determine to a great extent your success as a supervisor. **Respect** is the key word in all aspects of employee relations. The only thing that makes you, as owner, any different from your employees is the nature of your responsibilities.

Many employees have the potential to do just what you are doing. They have just not realized the possibilities, or perhaps their interests lie in other directions. Your employees may have knowledge and skills that would amaze you. So never speak condescendingly to them. A "superior" attitude is a good sign of an inferior manager. Who knows? One of your people may be a future partner — or competitor!

Treat your personnel with respect and they will reward you with a conscientious job and reliability. If you try to intimidate them, they will find ways to damage your accounts and create bad will for your company.

Your employees are really your company image. They are the people who will make or break you. A janitorial service is mainly selling labor. Your employees' work is your product, the yardstick by which a customer will judge you. So do what you must to motivate your employees and keep them working for you, not against you.

SHOW A PERSONAL INTEREST — An effective supervisor will show a personal interest in the welfare of each worker. So many contractors never bother to talk to an employee until they have got a complaint. This is poor policy.

Keep the line of communication open with all your employees. It's good for morale and you can learn a lot, too. Since they are doing the work day in and day out, they often know more about what's going on at their job site than you do. They may also have developed efficient short cuts on particular jobs that you will want to know about.

POSITIVE MOTIVATION involves praise for a job well done, appreciation for their effort, as well as whatever material benefits you are able to provide. Any benefits you can afford will pay for themselves.

If you see that an employee is punctual and reliable, do not take this for granted. Never take any positive action of an employee for granted. If you do, they will begin to feel that you do not appreciate their efforts, and they will either quit or stop trying.

PROVIDE AN OPPORTUNITY TO ADVANCE — Let's face it, a lot of maintenance personnel are not looking for a future in cleaning. They are just trying to make ends meet. But your best workers will **want** to feel there is a future with your company, an opportunity to advance. How do you keep these people?

If you are hiring employees, your business must be expanding and that means you are going to need supervisory help, sooner or later. If you have an exceptional employee, let him or her know that there will be an opportunity to advance. Start to identify and develop potential supervisors **before** you actually need them. Then when you get your first big account, you will be ready to take it on.

TRAINING — Employee motivation is interwoven with good training. People tend to dislike what they don't understand. They just turn it off. When employees fail to receive good initial training, they don't understand the job and they don't last long. Everyone needs to know what their job is all about and exactly what they are expected to do.

Being criticized for not doing a job right when you were never shown how to do it properly in the first place creates resentment. Being criticized for not performing a task when you were never even told that it was your responsibility will send you right through the roof!

To avoid alienating employees right off the bat, you have got to provide them with thorough training. This includes a complete on-site orientation on the account(s) they will be servicing. In training a new employee, don't take anything for granted. Certain facts may seem self-explanatory to you, but the employee may be totally unaware of them.

You can't train someone to do something that you don't know how to do yourself. The person doing the training, be it yourself or your supervisor, needs to be familiar with the particular account the employee is being trained for. It isn't enough to describe what needs to be done. It isn't even enough to show what should be done. You've got to **explain**, **demonstrate** and **work with** the new employee until he or she gets the hang of it. People learn by doing. On-the-job training is mandatory in this business. Never leave a new employee alone to do the work until **you** know that **they** know the job.

If at all possible, you should avoid training a new employee on a brand new account. Until you get familiar with the new building and develop an efficient system, you won't be able to properly train him or her. All you will do is create confusion. When the boss is going around in circles trying to figure out what to do, the employee starts to wonder.

CHECKING WORK — After the employee is trained and ready to handle the account alone, you must still check up on the work regularly. How often you check will depend on the frequency of the particular job and the reliability of the employee. Whether it is once a week or every night, you've got to inspect the work. This is called **quality control**. It's a matter of survival.

It is a good idea to check your accounts during the daylight hours or on the weekends to see how your employees are really doing. No matter how good the artificial lighting is, it does not show up the dirt in the same way that the sun does. Areas that appear clean to them at 10 p.m. may not look that way to the customer at 9 a.m.

This can be a real eye opener! And it will help you to identify areas that need more attention during the nightly cleaning.

CALL-IN SYSTEM — You can put new employees on a call-in system, especially if they are working an early morning account where oversleeping could cause problems. When they are ready to leave home just have them phone in: "I'm on my way." Either you or your answering service can verify that they are "awake and ready". This procedure will save you an account someday.

There are always reasons an employee cannot make it to work from time to time, but there should rarely if ever be a reason that the employee, or their spouse or a friend cannot call in.

Once the employee has proven his reliability you can take him off the phone-in requirement. Give him a raise too! Reliable employees are not that easy to find, so make sure they know you appreciate them getting the job done for you.

DEALING WITH POOR PERFORMANCE — When the quality of an employee's work drops off, you will have to bring it to his or her attention immediately. When you approach an employee about job quality it should be in a straightforward, constructive way — nothing devious. The challenge is to convince the employee that it is to his or her benefit as well as yours to get the job done right. Each person is unique and you need to learn to relate to each one in a way that gets through. This involves learning to see things from the employee's point of view.

Let your employee know in a firm but friendly way exactly what areas need improvement. Show that you still have confidence in him or her by finding something positive to say about the work that they are performing satisfactorily.

No matter how you approach the situation, you are bound to get some type of an excuse. That is human nature. You must listen carefully and determine if the employee has a legitimate problem. It may be that you are partly to blame for his inability to get the job done. Perhaps the time standard is unrealistic or maybe the employee isn't getting the supplies and equipment he needs. Perhaps he didn't receive adequate training, or maybe he hasn't been able to get hold of you on the phone to straighten out some difficulty.

Poor work is often a result of boredom. The employee may just have been doing the same thing for too long. A transfer to a new account might break the pattern and get things back on track.

Overworking is another cause of poor performance. Have you ever had a job where the harder you worked, the more work they gave you? If you have, then you shouldn't make that mistake when you become an employer. Don't overwork a good employee if you want to keep him.

Firing is your last resort. It isn't easy for anyone, but sometimes there is no other option. Dismissing an employee should be done in a civilized manner. Just tell the individual that it is not working out and you think you would be better off going your separate ways. Wish him the best of luck — life goes on.

EMPLOYEE TURNOVER — A considerable amount of turnover is a fact of life in maintenance work, so you might as well plan on it and get the best people you can at any given time. Your hiring practices can help reduce the turnover problem. Try to locate those people who really want and need the job.

Obviously you want to hire people who are going to stick around. Transients will be here today and gone tomorrow. You want to avoid hiring them, if possible. Hiring applicants who live too far from the job site is inviting trouble as well.

Certainly a part of the turnover problem can be traced back to poor management and supervision. An employee who is not given much respect, recognition or proper training has little reason to stay on the job. Who would?

A lot of people leave looking for more money. If you can afford to pay a little more than the other guys, then it will certainly help. Using a flat rate system (paying by account) where you can will definitely help.

You may find that you can minimize the effects of turnover by going mainly with part-time help, moonlighters in particular. It is much easier to find a replacement for a part-time employee who was doing two accounts than it is to replace a full-timer who was handling six accounts. In many cases one of your other part-timers will want more work and you won't need to hire anyone.

EMPLOYEE RECORDS

A personnel file should be set up for each new employee. In this file will go all paperwork related to that individual employee — job application, tax records, performance evaluations and employee's record of earnings, etc.

Each new employee you hire should fill out a **W-4 form**, which indicates the number of withholding allowances they are claiming. With the information on this form you will be able to withhold the correct amount of tax from his or her wages.

By January 31 of the following year you must provide each employee with a **W-2 form** (Wage and Tax Statement). You will also forward a copy of each W-2 to the Social Security Administration (SSA) along with a **W-3 form** (Transmittal of Income and Tax Statements). (See IRS Publication #15, "Employer's Tax Guide", Circular E , for details.)

In order to provide correct W-2 statements and meet federal laws, you must keep an accurate record of all employee wages, deductions, pay rates, etc. (See example, next page) You should keep these records for at least four years.

FEDERAL REGULATIONS

COMPLYING WITH THE IRCA — The Immigration Reform and Control Act (IRCA) of 1986 was designed to protect jobs for American citizens and legal aliens. In order to comply with the law you will need to get some copies of **Form I-9** (Employment Eligibility Verification). You can pick these up at any Immigration & Naturalization Service (INS) office. Also ask for a "Handbook for Employers", #M-274, which contains detailed information on the law as well as copies of Form I-9, which you can photocopy. I-9 Forms are also available at many stationery stores.

If there is no INS office in your area, you can call them toll free at 1-800-777-7700 for information. I-9 Forms can also be ordered in bulk by writing to the Superintendent of Documents, U.S. Government Printing Office, Washington, D.C. 20402. (Telephone 202-783-3238) Your local library may also have copies of the Employer Handbook.

The law requires you to complete Form I-9 for each new employee you hire. This applies to **anyone** you hire — even a family member. (You do not need to use I-9 Forms for subcontractors.) The directions on the back of the form are easy to understand and explain in detail what you must do. Basically, the law requires you, as an employer, to do five things:

1. Have your employees fill out and sign their part of Form I-9 within three business days of the date of hire. (If you employ the person for less than three days you must complete the Form I-9 before the end of the employee's first working day.)

2. Check the documents establishing the employee's identity and eligibility to work. (You do not have to verify the authenticity of these documents. Just check to see if they appear to be genuine and to relate to the person you are hiring.) It is a good idea to make a photocopy of these documents and save them along with the I-9 Form.

3. Complete and sign your portion of the Form I-9.

4. Keep the form on file for at least three years. (If the employee stays with you for more than three years, you should keep the form until one year after they leave your employment.)

EMPLOYEE RECORD OF EARNINGS

Name: George Smith   Soc. Sec. No.: 000-00-0000   Position: Janitor
Address: 11 Citrus Circle, Valley Center   Exemptions: Married — 1   Part-time:
Phone: 749-0000   Date Employed: April 17, 1989   Full time: V

PAYCHECK DATE	CHECK NUMBER	PAY PERIOD ENDING	HOURS Regular Hours	Rate	Overtime Hours	Rate	GROSS EARNINGS	FEDERAL INCOME TAX WITHHOLDING	F.I.C.A.	STATE INCOME TAX CALIFORNIA WITHHOLDING	S.D.I. (.009)	OTHER	NET PAY
April 21	1342	4-21	25	4.50			112 50	2 00	8 45	0	1 01		101 04
" 28	1354	4-28	30	4.50			135 00	6 00	10 14	0	1 22		117 64
May 5	1371	5-5	28	4.50			126 00	4 00	9 46	0	1 13		114 41
" 12	1386	5-12	26	4.50			117 00	3 00	8 79	0	1 05		104 16
" 19	1395	5-19	30	4.75			142 50	6 00	10 70	0	1 28		124 52
" 26	1411	5-26	25	4.75			118 75	3 00	8 92	0	1 07		105 76
June 2	1420	6-2	26	4.75			123 50	3 00	9 27	0	1 11		110 12

5. Have the form available for inspection by an INS or Department of Labor official upon request. (They must give you three days' advance notice.)

COMPLYING WITH OSHA — All employers must now comply with the Occupational Safety and Health Administration's (OSHA's) Hazard Communication Standard. Basically the law says that employees have a legal "Right-To-Know" about the health hazards of any chemicals they are required to use in their work.

This complex regulation requires, among other things, that you train your employees to use chemicals safely. And you must be sure that all containers of potentially harmful chemicals are properly labeled. You are also required to obtain and keep on file written Material Safety Data Sheets (MSDS's) from the manufacturer or vendor of any hazardous chemical product you use. (Ask your janitorial supplier.) A copy of the OSHA regulation is available through any OSHA office.

EMPLOYER TAXES

Your first step on the employer paperwork ladder is to file for an **employer identification number**. This is done on Form SS-4 available at any IRS office. There is no fee. Also request a copy of IRS Publication #15, "Employer's Tax Guide", Circular E.

Once you have applied for your employer I.D. number, you will be "in the system". The IRS will regularly send you the necessary forms and instructions, along with a number of their publications detailing your employer tax responsibilities.

The basic wage you pay your employees is just the beginning. As an employer there are federal and state taxes that you will be required to withhold from your employee's wages, along with a few additional taxes you must pay out of your own pocket.

Income tax withholding — You are required by the IRS to withhold federal income tax from your employees' wages. The tables used to determine the amount of employee withholding are available in IRS Publication #15, "Employer's Tax Guide", Circular E.

Social Security tax (FICA) — You must also withhold Social Security tax (FICA) from the employee's paycheck. As an employer you are required to **match** the Social Security tax withheld from your employees. For example, at the current FICA rate of 7.51%, if you pay an employee $100 you would have to

122

withhold $7.51 from his pay. You would also have to contribute $7.51 yourself, for a total contribution required of $15.02 (15.02%).

Reporting and depositing withheld taxes — You are required to report withheld income taxes and FICA taxes quarterly (every three months) to the IRS on Form 941. If the taxes you have withheld are less than $500 for the quarter, you can submit the entire amount along with Form 941.

If the taxes you have withheld are $500 or more (but less than $3,000) at the end of any month in the quarter, you must deposit the full amount by the 15th day of the next month. You must make your deposits at an authorized financial institution, usually your bank or a Federal Reserve Bank, using IRS Form 8109 "Federal Tax Deposit Coupon". (The IRS should send you a coupon book after you apply for your employer identification number. The coupons will be preprinted with your name, address and employer I.D. number.)

If the taxes you have withheld are over $3,000, there are special rules that apply. See IRS Publication #15, "Employer's Tax Guide", Circular E, for details.

Federal Unemployment tax (FUTA) — As an employer, you are responsible for paying Federal Unemployment tax. You cannot deduct it from your employee's wages. The current FUTA rate is 6.2% of wages paid during the year. The tax applies to the first $7,000 you pay each employee during the year.

Once a year (by January 31) you must file Form 940, "Employer's Annual Federal Unemployment (FUTA) Tax Return", along with your payment of tax due. (In some cases you may be required to make deposits during the year.) Once you have filed Form 940 the IRS will send you a preaddressed form each year. If you are a new employer, you will need to request Form 940 from the IRS.

Fortunately you can take a credit on Form 940 of up to 5.4% for amounts you pay to your state unemployment tax fund.

In addition to the federal employer taxes, you may also be required to pay various state taxes, such as unemployment tax. It is usually the same routine — apply for an I.D. number, get the information, withhold and pay taxes. Contact your state tax office for details.

There is no doubt that employer taxes are a burden, but there is one benefit — you can deduct them on your tax return at the end of the year.

WORKMEN'S COMPENSATION

Once you become an employer, you are required by law to carry a **Workmen's Compensation Insurance Policy** for your employees' protection on the job.

Workmen's Compensation rates are set in each state independently. The premiums are based on your total annual payroll. Rates vary according to how long you have been in business and the type of work you do. Generally, the more risk involved, the higher the rate. For example, you will pay a much higher rate on a window cleaner than on a secretary.

If you are a sole proprietor you will normally not be **personally** covered by your Workmen's Compensation Policy. If you are incorporated or in a partnership, you can usually get coverage for yourself as well as for your employees. A Workmen's Compensation Policy can usually be acquired through your insurance agent. If not, you may need to apply directly to your state Workmen's Compensation Board.

Chapter 8
SUBCONTRACTING

Subcontracting is defined as an "arrangement by which one who has contracted to do work gets it done for him by others under contract". When you subcontract you are working with independent contractors, rather than employees. Independent contractors may be individuals who work for themselves or companies with employees of their own.

SUBCONTRACTING OF SPECIALIZED WORK

General cleaning contractors often subcontract portions of their work to specialized companies. For example, if you have a building maintenance contract on a multi-story office building, you may subcontract with a window cleaning company to wash the exterior windows and with a carpet cleaning firm to clean the carpeting.

Tasks commonly subcontracted are carpet and upholstery cleaning, window cleaning, ceiling cleaning, pressure washing and parking lot sweeping. Cleaning companies often have informal agreements to subcontract or refer work to one another. One example is a commercial cleaning contractor who refers or subcontracts all residential work to a housecleaning company and vice versa.

Subcontracting of specialized tasks is becoming more and more common due to the cost of equipment and the special skill involved in handling certain types of cleaning. New contractors should have a business plan that defines what they **want** to do and what they **can** do. They should make arrangements to refer or subcontract the cleaning work they do not want.

FORM 1099-MISC

At the end of the year, you should complete an IRS Form 1099-Misc for each subcontractor you pay over $600. This form shows the subcontractor's name, address, social security number (or employer I.D. number) and the amount you paid. It serves the same purpose as the W-2's you give your employees.

You give one copy to the subcontractor by January 31st and send the other to the IRS by February 28th, along with a Transmittal Form 1096. You can get these forms along with an instruction pamphlet from the IRS.

SUBCONTRACTING JANITORIAL ACCOUNTS

Some cleaning contractors use subcontractors, rather than employees, to do the work on their regular janitorial accounts. The subcontractor is usually paid a percentage of the gross amount received by the contractor. This percentage is subject to negotiation between the two parties and, depending on the account, could range anywhere from 50% to 90%. The contractor takes the remaining percentage as his payment for managing the account, as well as for his initial efforts in securing the contract.

Payment is generally made on a monthly basis, with the subcontractor invoicing the contractor at the end of each month.

All the terms of the agreement between the contractor and the subcontractor should be spelled out clearly in a **written subcontract agreement** — job location, work specifications, contract amount, terms of payment, effective date, etc. A signed written agreement helps to avoid misunderstandings and problems down the road.

WHY SUBCONTRACT?

Why use subcontract labor rather than hire employees? There are a number of advantages.

Increased production — Many cleaning companies have found that they have been able to increase production by working primarily with independent contractors. Good subcontractors will take the same kind of interest in the account that you do, because they are not just working for an hourly wage. They are working to build up their own business.

No payroll tax expenses — There are virtually no payroll tax expenses involved in hiring subcontractors. Subcontractors pay their own taxes and provide their own insurance. They supply and maintain their own equipment and provide their own cleaning supplies. Your paperwork is reduced to a minimum

Improved cash flow — Cash flow problems are reduced because subcontractors are usually paid at the end of the month rather than weekly. This is especially beneficial to your cash flow on new accounts, because you do not have to cover those first few weekly payrolls right away. A fixed monthly subcontract allows for easy budgeting and planning.

Time off — Subcontracting is commonly used by one-man operations as a means to get time off, without having to hire and supervise employees. For example, a contractor with a seven-day-a-week account may hire a subcontractor to clean the account two or three days a week. This gives the contractor some time off and, if he has found a good sub, he won't have to worry about his account going down the drain in his absence.

Generally speaking, the best subcontractors are small, owner-operated businesses, or individuals just getting started. It is hard to find a worker with greater motivation than the man or woman who is dedicated to getting a small business off the ground.

WHAT CAN GO WRONG?

Although there are many advantages to working with subcontractors, this method of doing business is not without its drawbacks. Here are some of the disadvantages:

Loss of control — You cannot supervise a subcontractor the same way you would an employee. While subcontractors can act independently to your advantage, they also may "take matters into their own hands" at the wrong times.

Subcontracting works out best when the subcontractor is doing the work himself. Once he or she hires employees in your account your control over the actual work quality can be greatly reduced. It may also be more difficult to terminate a subcontractor than it would be to terminate an employee — depending on your agreement with the subcontractor, you may have to give 30 days' notice.

Subcontractors may steal your accounts — Independent contractors have been known to promote their own business interests at the expense of the contractor. Since the subcontractor is actually working at the account, he is the one the owner sees and gets to know. Your sub gets on a first name basis with the owner, does a few extras, and the next thing you know, he's got your account.

Customer resistance — Some potential customers may not want to award you the bid if they know you intend to use subcontractors. They don't want to lose control any more than you do!

Other customers may reason that if you can afford to hire a subcontractor they must be paying too much.

Insurance — You may have difficulty obtaining liability insurance to cover the work done by your subcontractors. You can also run afoul of the state Workmen's Compensation fund and the unemployment office.

What if your subcontractor quits, gets fired or injures himself on the job? He may apply to collect unemployment pay or Workmen's Compensation benefits, claiming he worked for you as an employee all along. You'll be in hot water for not paying unemployment taxes, and without Workmen's Compensation insurance, you could be liable for medical bills.

In any dispute with these government agencies the burden of proof will lie with you.

The Internal Revenue Service — Generally speaking, the IRS and other regulatory agencies don't encourage subcontracting. They are well aware that many employers call their employees "subcontractors" solely to avoid paying employment taxes. They would rather see you go the employment route — do all the paperwork, pay all the taxes and provide all the benefits.

EMPLOYEE OR INDEPENDENT CONTRACTOR?

Just calling a person a subcontractor does not make him one. According to the IRS, "If an employer-employee relationship exists, it does not matter what it is called. The employee may be called a partner, agent or independent contractor. It also does not matter how payments are measured or paid, what they are called, or whether the employee works full or part-time." (IRS Publication #15) In other words, an employee by any other name is still an employee!

When determining whether a worker is an employee or an independent contractor, the IRS (or other government agency) decides by the facts in each case. Here are some of the factors that are looked at:

When The Worker Is An Employee

1. The employer has the right to control or supervise the employee regarding what shall be done and how it shall be done.
2. The employer furnishes the tools and working location.
3. The employer has the right to fire the employee.

When The Worker Is An Independent Contractor

1. The worker is subject to the control of another only as to the final result to be accomplished by the work and not as to the means and method of accomplishing the result.

2. The worker sets his own hours, determines his own routine and may hire his own employees.
3. The worker offers his services to the public and other businesses as part of his own business.
4. The worker provides and maintains his own tools.
5. The worker receives payment by the job, not by the hour.
6. The worker provides his own insurance.

PROTECT YOURSELF

If you are going to hire subcontractors, go about it in the right way. **Protect yourself** by hiring only legitimate independent contractors, individuals who are clearly engaged in their own business.

Make sure they have a business license (if required), and carry their own insurance (including Workmen's Compensation if they have employees). Your subcontractors should own their own equipment and provide services to other customers. Your liability coverage should include work done by your subcontractors on your accounts. Have a written subcontract agreement that spells out your relationship as Contractor and Subcontractor, and be sure to send in the 1099 Forms at the end of the year.

Chapter 9
OFFICE CLEANING

Cleaning small and medium-sized offices is the easiest way to get started in contract cleaning. You can start with a small investment in equipment and there is less competition. You can also make more money per hour cleaning small offices than you can on larger accounts.

OFFICE CLEANING THE PROFESSIONAL WAY

Office cleaning is more of a skill than many people realize. A real professional goes through an office in a kind of flowing rhythm, very fast and efficient. No backtracking or standing around pondering what to do next. The saying "Time is money" was probably coined by a professional cleaner.

Your goal in office cleaning is not to sterilize and sanitize every nook and cranny of a building, no matter how long it takes. Your objective is to provide the specific services your customer is paying for at a level of quality that is acceptable, and you must accomplish this in a time frame that allows you to make a profit.

The trick to making good money in office cleaning lies in developing highly efficient work routines. This allows you to do the work faster and better than your competitors.

DEVELOPING EFFICIENT OFFICE CLEANING ROUTINES

Work routines are far more important in this line of work than in most others. In the janitorial business, where up to 90% of your operating expense is labor, it is essential to have an efficient routine worked out for each account. In many cases the efficiency of the work routine will make the difference between just breaking even on an account or making a decent profit.

It takes practice and some creativity to discover the optimum way to get a particular office cleaned. Once you get the knack you will be able to clean offices rapidly and develop an efficient routine on any job in a short period of time.

The ideal routine on each account will vary according to the building size, design and the cleaning required. But no matter what the job is, the main enemies are wasted motion and lost time.

There are two parts to an office cleaning routine. First, you must choose the most efficient cleaning path or route through the building. The best path is the one that requires the least amount of steps and backtracking. Second, you must perform all the basic cleaning tasks (trashing, dusting and vacuuming) in a logical sequence.

The professional cleaner works around an office in a circular, clockwise direction, emptying and cleaning ashtrays, dumping the trash, dusting, spot cleaning and vacuuming in that order. Depending on the size of the office and the cleaning system employed, this will take two or three passes (or loops) around the office.

Most smaller offices are cleaned in two passes. First, you go around the room cleaning ashtrays, dumping the trash, dusting and spot cleaning. On the second pass you vacuum.

Large office buildings are often cleaned using a team system, which requires three passes through the office — one person trashing, another dusting and spot cleaning, and a third vacuuming. For more on this system of cleaning, see "Cleaning Large Office Buildings" later in this chapter.

Whenever possible you should carry all the cleaning supplies you need and still leave both hands free. A spray bottle of glass cleaner, a spray bottle of all-purpose detergent, a clean cloth and a treated dust cloth take care of 95% of routine cleaning. These items can be easily carried on your belt, in an apron pocket, or on a trash cart or rolling trash can.

Some jobs, like restroom cleaning, will require more tools and supplies. Then you can use a caddy (a small basket) or a janitor's cart. When you use a cart or caddy, always move it along with you or leave it in the most central or accessible location, to cut down on the back and forth time. This "to and fro" activity breaks your cleaning rhythm and slows you down. Eliminate it whenever possible.

Each portion of a cleaning job should flow smoothly into the next. Backtracking and erratic cleaning routes are a waste of time and money. People who make cleaning their profession know that the word "rhythm" has a lot to do with it. A real pro makes it look easy — and it is easy! It's like any other occupation. The more you practice, the faster and more proficient you become.

OFFICE CLEANING EQUIPMENT AND SUPPLIES

It takes just a few supplies and a very small investment to get started in office cleaning. Here is a list of the basic equipment you will need:

Vacuum cleaner — The commercial upright vacuum is generally regarded by contractors as the best all-around machine for routine carpet care. It cleans deeper than the cannister-type machine because the brush (beater bar) located in the front of the vacuum intake continuously combs the carpet, loosening the dirt and drawing it into the vacuum.

Upright vacuums are measured by the length of the beater brush. A vacuum with a 12" to 16" brush is a good size for all-around use. The larger the brush the faster the work can be done. Prices on new 12" machines start at about $150 and 16" machines start at about $200.

Vacuums for commercial use should have a permanent cloth bag (rather than a disposable paper one) and an adjustable depth control for different types of carpeting.

It is a good idea to carry a back-up vacuum in your vehicle — any old, inexpensive machine that you can turn to if your commercial vacuum breaks down in the middle of a job. Most household vacuums do not have the power or durability for regular maintenance work, but are adequate as a back-up.

Trash containers on wheels — Depending on the job requirements, you can use a large trash can on wheels, a janitor's cart (maid's cart) or a folding waste cart (a bag suspended from a tubular steel frame on wheels).

Treated dust cloths — You can use the pretreated disposable cloths or you can treat your own with a dust control product such as Dust Up or Endust.

Cleaning cloths — Small cotton terry towels for spot cleaning in office areas, and for wiping and polishing fixtures, chrome and mirrors in restrooms.

Spray bottle of all-purpose detergent — Buy a good quality, all-purpose neutral detergent. Dilute it in water in a medium-sized plastic trigger spray bottle (24 oz. size). Used for spot cleaning.

Spray bottle of glass cleaner — Dilute a little glass cleaner in a 24 oz. trigger spray bottle. Used for spot cleaning entry door glass, office partitions and restroom mirrors.

Furniture polish — Protects and enhances the appearance of natural wood surfaces. Don't overdo it or the polish will build up and dull the finish. Never use on glass — it streaks and leaves a film that is difficult to remove.

Lamb's wool dusting wand — Used for quick dusting of high and low places, venetian blinds and other irregular surfaces.

Carpet spot cleaner — Used as necessary to keep the carpet looking good on a daily basis. (See Chapter 11)

Trash can liners — Plastic liners keep waste baskets clean and sanitary.

OFFICE CLEANING PROCEDURES

The four basic duties in office cleaning are trashing (removing the trash), dusting, vacuuming and restroom cleaning.

TRASHING

Trashing involves collecting and removing the trash from the building. How you collect and remove the trash depends somewhat on the size of the building. In small offices you can simply carry a large plastic trash bag as you go from waste basket to waste basket. But when you dump trash this way you must be careful not to throw in any liquids from half-full coffee cups and soda pop cans. These can leak out and spot the carpeting.

In larger buildings you will need some type of waste receptacle on wheels to collect the trash and carry your basic cleaning supplies. You can use a janitor's cart, a folding waste cart or a plastic trash can on wheels.

To hold your supplies, you can buy a wrap-around canvas caddy which attaches to the handles of the trash can. Or you can simply hang your spray bottles and cleaning cloths from the rim of the can. Be sure to carry a supply of the different size plastic liners you will need. These can be carried in a bag hung from the side of the can. You should also keep a roll of large trash bags in the bottom of the can for quick replacement. Now you have everything you need right at hand as you move from desk to desk.

As you empty the wastebaskets check the liners. If they are dirty, replace them. Be sure to put the wastebaskets back where you found them. Don't throw away anything that isn't already in the trash. Empty boxes and other items sitting next to trash cans are not necessarily trash — when in doubt, leave them!

Ashtrays should be dumped and wiped clean as you trash. Lower the ashtray into the trash bag and **gently** turn it over, or you will have ashes flying about landing on the desks. Ashtrays may be wiped clean with a damp cloth or paper towel then wiped dry, leaving no streaks. If they are very dirty you can clean them with steel wool, the fine grade.

Be sure you aren't putting any smoldering cigarettes in with the waste paper. It is a good idea to have a small metal container, such as a coffee can, attached to your trash cart for the hot ashes.

Be especially cautious emptying trash cans around copy machines. Every so often someone dumps toner (black powder) in the trash can. This powder is very fine and stains everything it touches. If you dump it out the toner will fly all over the room, settling on the desks, paperwork, carpet — everywhere. If you see any black powder on the trash can liner, **tie the bag off** and throw the whole thing out.

While you are trashing, be sure to pick up any loose litter or paper clips lying about. It will speed up your vacuuming later. When you have filled the trash container pull the bag out, tie it off and leave it in a convenient spot (off the carpeting) for removal to the dumpster.

Some buildings have special procedures regarding trash removal. You should check on this before starting work. For instance, as a security measure banks often save the trash from the teller stations for several days or a week. This trash should be collected in a small bag, held out separately and stored in a designated area.

DUSTING

For regular dusting you can use the disposable pretreated cloths or treat your own cloth with a dust control aerosol.

When you dust make sure you put everything back exactly where it was. Clients don't like to see their desks "reorganized" each night. You can straighten and tidy items such as nameplates, ashtrays and telephones, but it is usually best to leave the paperwork right where it lies. Pick up the papers and dust underneath them, then set them back where they were. As messy as it all may look to you, it probably means something to someone just the way it is.

While you are dusting you should also take care of any general cleaning that needs to be done, such as spot cleaning the desktops for coffee spills, etc. Watch for smudges and fingerprints on desks, furniture, phones, glass partitions, woodwork, around door knobs and light switch plates.

Depending on the surface you can use the all-purpose cleaner, glass cleaner or furniture polish. For cleaning ink marks off formica desks or counters, acetone works when nothing else will. If your janitorial supplier does not carry it, you can buy it at almost any hardware store. Acetone is a solvent, so use proper care.

As you dust and clean the desks, pull the chairs out. This will make your vacuuming job easier. Keep your eye out for carpet spots as you go — it is easier to remove them now than when you are vacuuming.

HIGH/LOW DUSTING

Periodically you will need to take care of the detail dusting or high/low dusting. This includes the tops of partitions, door and window mouldings, picture frames, baseboards, chair legs, etc. The best tool for high/low dusting is a lamb's wool dusting wand. Lamb's wool is a natural dust collector. Just lightly brush the wand over the area and it "grabs" the dust. It works well on venetian and mini blinds too.

One good way of handling the detail dusting is to do a little bit each day. That way when the job comes due it has already been done. For instance, if your contract calls for the dusting of venetian blinds monthly in a building with 25 offices, this will be quite a chore to do all at once. However, if you perform this required dusting in just one office per night, you will hardly feel it and at the end of the month all the work has been done.

VACUUMING

Vacuuming comes last, after trashing and dusting. Some janitors advise vacuuming first, reasoning that the vacuuming will stir up dust. However, on most jobs there is small litter to be dusted off the desks, and trashing and emptying ashtrays is often messy, so you must vacuum last to wind up with a professional-looking job. Also "vacuuming yourself out the door" leaves the carpeting without any footprints — a nice psychological effect.

For daily vacuuming of office carpeting, the most popular machine is the upright commercial vacuum, the 12" to 16" size with variable depth setting. Uprights are used in a push and pull fashion; each stroke should partially overlap the previous one. The depth setting should be set so that the beater bar moves the carpet pile without digging in too deep. If the vacuum is hard to push, the setting is too low. If the vacuum isn't lifting the pile and leaving a track on the carpet, the setting is too high.

It is usually best to work from the back of the office toward the front. Walk backward with the upright so that you are not constantly tracking on the area you have just vacuumed. Be sure to vacuum under the desks (the chairs should already be pulled out). As you finish vacuuming under each desk, push the chair back, being careful not to bang it on the furniture. Once you get the knack you will find yourself using one hand to vacuum while using the other hand, and sometimes your foot, to move the furniture.

Be sure to empty the bag often. The machine will pick up much better when the bag isn't stuffed. Also check the belt on the beater bar regularly as they get stretched out and occasionally break. When you check the belt also look at the beater bar and remove any string or thread that may be tangled there. Keep an extra belt or two looped over the vacuum handle, in case one breaks.

When the machine picks up a hard object, tip the machine back slightly and the object will usually pop out. If it doesn't, turn off the machine immediately, or you risk breaking the fan in the motor. For safety's sake never put your hand under the machine while it is turned on. Also avoid running over the cord and never vacuum a wet carpet.

If you move anything while vacuuming, be sure you get it back in its usual place before you leave. To avoid backtracking, flip off the light switches as you vacuum from one area to the next. Before you turn out the lights, stop for a second and glance around the room. How does it look? Everything in order?

DETAIL VACUUMING

Periodically you will need to detail vacuum or "edge" the carpeting, to clean the places where the upright can't reach — along the baseboards, in corners and under furniture.

The best way to do this is with an edging or crevice tool attachment on a cannister vacuum, tank vacuum or backpack type vacuum. If you don't have this type of equipment you can do a respectable job with a small broom such as a lobby broom. Just go along the edges and sweep the litter out far enough for the upright to pick it up.

RESTROOM CLEANING

When you first go into a new building, you may have to spend extra time getting the restrooms back up to a sanitary and bright appearance. Once they are up to par it will be easy to keep them that way.

Restrooms are not an area to cut corners in. Clients and customers are rarely oblivious to the sanitation of their restrooms. In fact, some people will judge your entire maintenance operation by this one area alone.

RESTROOM CLEANING SUPPLIES

In small offices with just a few restrooms you can carry your restroom cleaning supplies in a caddy. In large office buildings you will find that a cart is necessary. Here are the basic supplies you will need:

Disinfectant restroom cleaner — Comes in aerosol or liquid for mixing in a trigger spray bottle. Used for cleaning and sanitizing restroom fixtures and other surfaces.

Bowl mop and acid cleaner — Used periodically for sanitizing toilets.

Hand scrubbing pads — White scouring sponges used for cleaning sinks. Use the mildly abrasive ones that will not scratch the chrome. Don't use scouring powder. It can scratch surfaces and is hard to rinse away.

Caddy or maid cart — Used to hold and transport restroom cleaning supplies. Use a caddy on small accounts, a maid's cart on large ones.

Brooms, mops, buckets and wringers and other floor cleaning supplies will be needed for the hard floors in restrooms. (See Chapter 12)

Pumice stick — Used to remove toilet bowl rings and mineral deposits. Works when nothing else will.

Cleaning supply aprons — Are useful for carrying spray bottles and other cleaning supplies. May be worn, or attached to the side of a folding waste cart.

RESTROOM CLEANING METHODS

It is a good idea to empty the trash, refill the dispensers and sweep the floor before starting on the sinks and toilets. This prevents any loose dirt on the floor from turning to mud if you splash or drip water while cleaning the fixtures. Sometimes, depending on the building design, it may be easier to sweep the restrooms while you are sweeping the rest of the building.

Spray cleaning is the fastest way to clean a restroom. You can use a store-bought industrial aerosol such as Dow Bathroom Cleaner, or you can use a trigger spray bottle containing a disinfectant detergent. Spray the surfaces to be cleaned and then dry them to a shine with paper towels or a clean cloth.

If the sinks are very dirty use a white scrub sponge. Don't use an abrasive powdered cleaner. It is time-consuming to use, difficult to rinse away thoroughly and, if used regularly, may dull the enamel surface. All mirrors, stainless steel and chrome should be shined spotlessly, leaving no streaks. But don't do this until you have cleaned the sink — otherwise you will just be getting more water spots on them.

Toilets and urinals should be cleaned on the outsides with spray cleaner and paper towels or clean cloths. Seats should be sprayed and wiped clean on both sides. It is standard practice to leave the toilet seat up after cleaning.

Bowl cleaner should be used only as necessary. Don't pour the acid cleaner right into the water. First use your bowl mop to force the water out of the bowl. (Use the mop like a plunger.) You don't need to push all the water out of the bowl — just push out enough so it drops down below its usual level.

Apply the bowl cleaner directly to the mop and spread the undiluted acid around the inside of the bowl. Be careful not to splash it around. It is an acid and can cause damage to all kinds of surfaces, including your hands and eyes.

When you use bowl cleaner, be sure to apply it first thing when you start in the restroom. That way it can work while you are doing the other cleaning. When you have finished cleaning the restroom, flush the bowl cleaner away.

If there is still a ring in the toilet bowl even after using the acid cleaner, you can use a **pumice stick** to remove it. Wet the end of the stick and use it as you would an eraser.

It isn't necessary to clean all the restroom partitions and walls each night. But you should **spot clean** around the toilets and urinals and around and underneath the dispensers. Also touch up the areas where people put their hands — around door handles, stall doors, light switches, etc.

It is important to check each tissue, towel and soap dispenser every time you clean. Keep them well stocked — empty dispensers are the cause of most restroom complaints.

If there is an odor problem, don't rely on deodorants and room fresheners. Use an acid-based bowl cleaner frequently in toilets and urinals, and mop the floors daily with a detergent containing a disinfectant. Also clean the trash can itself periodically with a disinfectant. Pour a disinfectant solution down drains from time to time.

Keep an eye on the high dusting — the tops of partitions, mirrors, ceiling vents and light fixtures. Wipe clean the towel, soap and tissue dispensers. Don't forget the baseboards when you are cleaning the floor. Last but not least, remember to turn the light out if required.

IMPORTANT OFFICE CLEANING PRIORITIES

Learn to see a building from the client's point of view. What areas do they use most frequently? What is the first thing they notice on coming in in the morning? Where do people put their hands and what do they see when they glance about the room? These are areas you should pay particular attention to.

Entrances are always of special importance. The entrance appearance gives a customer his first impression of a business. An account may be in great shape elsewhere, but if the entry area is poorly maintained the overall impression will be unfavorable.

If the entry doors are plate glass, they should be spot-cleaned daily using glass cleaner. This only takes a few seconds.

The floor at the entrance receives tremendous wear from the constant tracking in of dirt. The incoming grit works like sandpaper on hard floors and creates a traffic lane in carpeting. This floor area will require the most care. If you can convince the owner to put down a walk-off mat at the entrance, much of the soil will be trapped before it gets into the building. This will protect the permanent flooring.

Other critical areas are restrooms, executive offices and desks and any clearly visible flat surfaces that collect dust quickly. Ashtrays, mirrors and glass table tops should be kept spotless. Watch for fingerprints around door knobs, light switch plates, office partitions and other areas where people put their hands. Trash cans and liners should be kept clean as well as empty.

Telephones and other small electronic and mechanical devices are often overlooked by the cleaner, but not by the client. These are the tools they work with constantly. Keep the dust and smudges off them.

If you have a janitor's closet or storage room at an account, make sure it is kept in good order. The appearance of this room says something about your company. If your supplies and equipment are in disorder, the customer may well conclude that your company is in the same condition.

You will find that regardless of what your agreement specifies, the building owner or manager always seems to have a few "sore spots" where the cleaning is concerned. These items may seem of secondary importance to you, but you had better put them at the top of your list of cleaning priorities if you want to keep the account for long.

SECURITY TIPS

When cleaning alone in a building after hours, always lock yourself in. If you go out to your truck or to the dumpster for a few minutes, lock the door behind you. If someone comes in and walks off with a typewriter or a computer, you will have to answer for it.

If you break anything or notice something unusual, leave a note for the manager and call or visit the next day.

When leaving any building, double check that the lights are off and the door is locked. Double checking a door means: Lock it and load your equipment into your vehicle. Then walk back and **try the door again.** If you get in the habit of doing this, you won't absent-mindedly leave a door open.

CLEANING SMALL OFFICES

When cleaning small offices on a route, you will usually have to carry in all your equipment and supplies each night. Many small offices provide little or no space for cleaning supplies. To save time you should try to bring in everything you need in one trip. With a well-organized caddy you can carry all your basic cleaning supplies in one hand and your vacuum in the other.

The basic items you will need on most small jobs are a spray bottle of all-purpose cleaner, a spray bottle of glass cleaner, bathroom cleaner, several clean cloths, a dust cloth, furniture polish, scrub pad, carpet spotter, small trash can liners and several large trash bags. You will also occasionally need a bowl mop, bowl cleaner, a lamb's wool duster and a pumice stick.

Small offices are usually cleaned by just one or two people. When you get three or more workers cleaning in a small space they start to get in each other's way, resulting in wasted time and reduced efficiency.

When you are cleaning alone you usually do the trashing and dusting together as one step, and then vacuum. You can clean the restrooms first or last, whichever works out best. In very small restrooms you can often spray everything that needs to be cleaned in one step, then wipe everything down in a second step. Rather than damp mopping the floor, you can clean it quickly with a damp cloth.

When two people are working the job, a good routine is for one person to start right in on the restrooms while the other begins trashing and dusting. Then, by the time the restrooms are cleaned, the trasher will be far enough ahead so that the one who has done the restrooms can begin vacuuming, working behind the trasher.

If the cleaning routine is worked out well, the trasher should just be finishing up his portion of the work as the vacuumer comes right in behind him. There should be no wasted time with one person sitting around waiting for the other to finish.

Of course every building and worker are different, so you will need to adjust the workload accordingly. There are always extra cleaning chores which one or the other can do to balance out the workload.

CLEANING LARGE OFFICE BUILDINGS

There are basically two ways to clean in larger office buildings — area cleaning and team cleaning.

Area cleaning — This is the same type of cleaning you do on your smaller accounts. But instead of one person cleaning an entire building, he or she may be assigned to clean just one floor or section.

Most janitors prefer area cleaning. They like to have an area where they can see the finished result, take pride in it and develop a sense that "this is my area". When area cleaning is employed, many contractors still utilize special crews for the restrooms and the project work like floor waxing. Periodic general cleaning tasks like high and low dusting are usually incorporated into the regular cleaners' routine.

Team cleaning — In team cleaning, instead of working in a specific area a cleaner is assigned a specific task, such as trashing or vacuuming. In a typical team cleaning system, the person assigned to trashing starts on the top floor of the building with a rolling trash can. He goes from desk to desk just emptying the trash and ashtrays. As the trash is collected from each floor he drops down to the next. The cleaner assigned to dusting and general cleaning starts in behind the trasher, following the same cleaning route. Next comes the vacuumer, again following the same pattern. Meanwhile a restroom crew is busy on the restrooms. Another team member may be assigned to detail vacuuming.

With proper training and organization a team cleaning system will yield greater production rates in a given building than area cleaning. Training is simplified because each new employee need only learn one skill to get started. As time goes on each employee can learn the other phases and rotate from one job to the next. This relieves boredom and provides more flexibility.

However, team cleaning also has its drawbacks. For a team system to work efficiently the trasher must move ahead unlocking doors and turning lights on. These doors are left open and the lights left on, so that the dusters and vacuumers can move through quickly. This can cause security and energy problems. Also, when many people are cleaning in the same area it is difficult to pinpoint responsibility for damaged or stolen property. Morale and personnel problems can develop as workers' responsibilities overlap and personalities get in the way of teamwork.

Area cleaning and team cleaning both have their place. Which system you use will depend on many factors: the size of the building, building design, cleaning required, management, security and energy requirements and your own personnel and management capabilities. On many accounts you will use a combination of the two — area cleaning for the office space and specialized teams for the restrooms and project work.

THE LONGER YOU CLEAN A PLACE THE SMALLER IT GETS

When you first start to clean a new account, it may seem to take a long time. This is natural — you are just getting oriented. Don't be discouraged. Each day you will find little ways to speed the work up. Before long you will be amazed at how quickly and easily you are accomplishing the work that at first was so time-consuming.

A good cleaning routine becomes so familiar and efficient that it is almost automatic. The longer you clean a place, the smaller it gets!

BE AN INNOVATOR

There are always ways to improve on any job. The really successful cleaning contractor is always on the alert for a better way, a new product or method that can save time and money. You may see an innovative way to get the work done faster, better and at a lower price than your competitors. It isn't enough just to do a job "the way it's always been done".

Be fast, be thorough, pay attention to detail and take pride in your work. Then find and train other people who can do the same. When you have accomplished that you will be on your way to great success in this business.

Chapter 10
WINDOW CLEANING

Although window cleaning is considered a specialized service, many janitorial companies include it as one of the regular services they offer. Basically there are two types of window cleaning — "high rise" (three stories and up) and "low work" (ground level and jobs that can be reached with an extension pole or ladder). High rise window cleaning takes training by an expert, a substantial investment in specialized equipment, and a certain kind of individual who likes to hang off the tops of tall buildings.

Low work takes a very small investment in equipment and can be learned by anyone who is willing to work at it. Low work is where all window cleaners start out and it is what this chapter is about.

WINDOW CLEANING EQUIPMENT

It takes a very small investment to get started in window cleaning. You can buy the basic start-up equipment for less than $50. But you should buy the very best quality tools available. The difference in price between the top-of-the-line squeegee and an average one is only a few dollars, but there is a world of difference in the quality of work you can produce, and in the time it takes you to do it.

BASIC EQUIPMENT AND SUPPLIES

Squeegees — Are used to dry the window after it has been cleaned. You need several lengths for different size glass surfaces. Three useful sizes are 8", 14" and 18". There are several types of squeegees. Most have interchangeable channels which allow the use of any length of squeegee blade on one handle.

Many professional cleaners prefer the brass squeegees to stainless steel or aluminum. They are a little more expensive but they last for a lifetime. The Ettore and Unger brand of squeegees have long been favorites of many professional window cleaners.

Strip washers — Are especially useful and timesaving tools for cleaning windows. The strip washer consists of a fabric sleeve that snaps on over a lightweight T-shaped handle. Strip washer sleeves come in different textures, from soft to rough, for routine to heavy cleaning. Strip washers come in lengths from 10" to 22".

The strip washer holds water well, allowing you to clean several windows without rewetting. This is especially important when you are working on a ladder.

Pail — To start with, any large plastic pail will do. Five gallon chemical containers work well. Some janitorial supply stores have empty ones for sale. But if you are planning on cleaning a lot of windows, it is worth the money to buy one of the long, rectangular-shaped buckets. These have room to hold a strip washer.

Squeegee holster — Very useful, because you have to have a place to put your squeegee while you are cleaning the window with the strip washer. You can also purchase a double holster, which has an extra slot to hold a second squeegee or strip washer.

Window scraper — An inexpensive paint scraper (razor blade and holder), available at hardware stores, is adequate for small jobs. For a lot of scraping or new construction work, get a professional quality window scraper with a 4" to 6" blade.

Drying towels — For drying squeegee and window edges. You need towels that are fairly lint-free. New or used cotton towels work well.

Window brush — Used for cleaning exterior windows. Unless you are going to be cleaning a lot of windows right away, you don't need the expensive boar's hair brush. Nylon or horsehair will do to start.

It used to be that every professional window cleaner used a brush for exterior windows. But since the strip washers came on the market, more and more window cleaners have switched to using them exclusively for both inside and outside windows. For exterior windows where you need more scrubbing power, a strip washer with a rough surface on one side (such as the Unger Ruf-Face) works well.

Window cleaning solution — Each professional window cleaner has his or her own idea about what solution cleans windows best. Some add a little ammonia, others use a pinch of TSP or a little alcohol. Some swear by a particular brand of dishwashing detergent. There are also specially formulated window cleaning solutions available at janitorial supply stores.

A good all-around cleaning solution is a small capful (¹/₂ teaspoon) of neutral **nonsudsing** detergent in a five gallon pail of warm water. Two household detergents that work well are Joy dishwashing liquid and Amway L.O.C. Just a squirt in a five gallon pail will do. For especially dirty windows or smoke film, you can add approximately three tablespoons (two ounces) of full-strength, odorless ammonia. Add the ammonia and detergent after you fill the pail (one half to three quarters full).

Whatever you do, don't use a high-sudsing detergent You will have streaks forever. Use just a little cleaning solution. The water really does most of the cleaning. The detergent is added to help spread and hold the water evenly on the glass and to dislodge any tough dirt or grease.

WINDOW CLEANING ACCESSORIES

Swivel action squeegees and strip washers — Tools with pivoting handles (like the Ettore Super System) save considerable time and allow you to reach areas that are difficult to clean with the conventional tools. Although a fairly recent innovation, the swivel action squeegees and strip washers are already considered a part of basic equipment by many window cleaners.

Ladders — Step ladders, from 5 to 8 feet in height, are useful on many jobs. You can use wood or aluminum, whichever you prefer. Extension ladders, from 13 to 50 feet, or sectional ladders from 6 to 26 feet, are used for work above the first story. Don't skimp — buy sturdy, extra heavy-duty ladders.

Extension poles — Telescoping poles are used to reach higher windows, up to 30 feet.

Natural or synthetic sponges — Can be used in place of a strip washer for inside and small panes. They are also useful for wiping window ledges and squeegee blades.

Chamois — Used for cleaning and drying windows and squeegee blades. Preferred over towels by some window cleaners.

WINDOW CLEANING TECHNIQUES

Window cleaning is one maintenance task that is more of an art than a job. A real professional makes it look so easy, but when you don't know the tricks of the trade it can be frustrating. Once you have mastered the technique, you will find the work satisfying and profitable.

The whole key to making money in window cleaning is doing the work quickly, so that you make an excellent hourly income. The more you do, the faster you get.

BASIC TECHNIQUE

First apply the solution to the entire surface of the window with the strip washer and work it around for a few seconds. Make sure you get all along the edges and into the corners. (When washing on the inside of the building be sure to hold the strip washer over the pail and squeeze off the excess water first, so you don't drip on the floor.) Place the strip washer back in the bucket and pull the squeegee from your holster.

The first step in using the squeegee is to "cut the water" (dry the edge) across the top of the window. You do this by placing the squeegee blade at the top edge of the window pane **on a slight angle** to the glass and drawing it all the way across the top. This gives you a dry edge, one or two inches wide, to work from. Wipe the squeegee blade dry with the towel or chamois.

Now simply dry the rest of the pane using downward strokes, each one starting on the dry strip, overlapping each stroke a few inches. Don't press too hard! After each stoke, be sure to dry the squeegee blade. In this technique, you should always start each stroke with a dry blade against dry glass, otherwise you will get streaks.

If the sill or some other obstacle prevents you from bringing your stroke all the way down, leave a wet strip along the bottom. At the end, cut the water on the vertical edge and clean off the bottom with one last stroke.

The same process can be performed horizontally, first cutting the water down the vertical edge, then making your strokes crossways.

Once you have finished be sure to wipe the dirty water off the sill, using a sponge or towel, without touching the glass. Any spots or streaks should be touched up using a lint-free towel or chamois. Wipe your towel quickly all along the edge of the pane to put the final touch on the job.

Don't be surprised or discouraged if your first efforts are a bit awkward or slow. Once you have had a little practice you will be able to work two to three times faster than you could at the start.

ADVANCED TECHNIQUE

Once you feel comfortable with the squeegee, you can gradually learn the more advanced technique of cleaning windows in one continuous stroke, without removing the squeegee from the glass. This is a much faster method and tends to leave less streaks.

In this technique you start in the left upper corner (if you are right-handed) and cut the water along the vertical edge. Next, start the stroke across the top of the window. As you approach the right corner, angle the tip of the squeegee all the way into the corner. Now without stopping, go down the side part way and turn the squeegee back in by making a quick half-turn with your wrist. Go back across the glass, overlapping the first stroke (by about two inches) and reverse your wrist again on the opposite side. Continue back and forth across the glass, working your way down. As you approach the bottom, angle the squeegee into the corner and finish with one last swipe across the bottom. Don't stop or break your rhythm at any point along the way. It should be one continuous stroke. The whole process can be described as a sort of fanning, "S"-shaped motion.

If done properly, the entire glass is clean with no streaks or missed areas. An experienced professional can clean a sheet of glass in this way in a matter of seconds. The trick lies in keeping the right pressure on the squeegee and learning to rotate your wrist smoothly as you swing the squeegee back and forth across the glass. You may find it helpful to hold the squeegee more with your fingers and thumb than in the palm of your hand. Don't try to go too fast in the beginning.

Many window cleaners find it easier to use a shorter squeegee blade in this technique, 12" to 14", as opposed to 16" to 24" used in the basic technique. The constant turning back and forth of the squeegee can cause strain on the elbow and wrist when using a longer blade, something similar to tennis elbow.

Don't be discouraged if you can't clean in a single stroke right away. No one can! It takes a good deal of practice to get the feel of the squeegee and to develop a cleaning rhythm. This is a skill that cannot be learned directly out of a book. It is like learning to ride a bicycle — it seems impossible at first, then as you keep trying, all of a sudden you start to get the knack. Practice is the only way.

There is no question that the "old pros" of window cleaning are very skilled and incredibly fast, but even a novice can learn to use the basic technique in a short period of time and make excellent money at window cleaning.

WINDOW CLEANING TIPS

1. To clean windows effectively, you must use a sharp squeegee blade. Even a little nick or rough spot on the edge of the rubber will allow water to slip under and leave little thin streaks. When your blade gets dull, reverse it. When both sides are dull, throw it away and replace it with a new sharp blade. Buying good quality squeegee blades (such as the Ettore brand) is the best investment any window cleaner can make.

2. If you are getting a lot of "tails" (dirt spots that streak when you squeegee), then you are probably not washing the window well enough. Squeegeeing is not a cleaning, but a **drying** process. Spend a little more time in scrubbing with the washing tool.

3. Try to avoid washing windows in the direct sunlight or in a strong wind. The water will evaporate before you can get the squeegee on it. During the summer, early morning and evening are the best, or try to time your work so that you stay in the shade.

4. In very cold or freezing weather you can use alcohol in your cleaning solution. It will help prevent the cleaning solution from freezing on the glass.

5. Be extremely careful of plexiglass or specially coated windows. These scratch very easily. Do not use a strong detergent or brush. Clean gently with a strip washer and plain warm water. Squeegee very lightly. Whatever you do, don't scrape them with a razor blade. There are specially formulated cleaners for plexiglass or solar coating available at janitorial supply stores.

6. Be careful when cleaning interior windows using an ammonia solution. If you splash it about it will "strip" little areas of waxed floor or polished wooden sills.

7. Always clean upper windows before lower ones. On very large windows, do one section of the glass at a time, upper sections first.

SAFETY TIPS

1. In washing and drying windows, **do not press too hard**, especially on large sheets of glass, or on cracked glass.

2. **If you use ammonia** in your cleaning solution remember that it is highly toxic. Never inhale the fumes directly.

3. **Ladder safety** — Never sacrifice safety for speed or expediency! Don't attempt to clean any windows from a ladder if you don't feel secure. Use an extension pole or find some other way. Never lean a ladder directly against the glass or on a frame that might give way. Don't stand on the top two rungs of a ladder. Be careful not to reach out too far, throwing the ladder off balance.

REMOVING HARD WATER SPOTS

From time to time you will encounter windows which have hazy mineral deposits or "hard water spots." These will not come off with ordinary cleaning and they cannot be scraped off. You can purchase a product (acid solution) especially designed for this purpose at a janitorial supply store, or through one of the national suppliers. Follow the instructions on the label of the product you are using for exact cleaning directions.

Usually it is best to apply the acid solution undiluted. Pour some out on a white scrub pad and spread it around on the window, being careful not to splash it about. Let it set for a few seconds, then work it in with the scrubbing pad. Don't use your regular cleaning tools for this. Some acid solutions are greasy and will streak the windows if they get in your regular wash water.

After you have scrubbed the window, wipe the acid cleaner off as thoroughly as possible with a towel. Then rinse and clean the windows as usual with your regular wash water. The spots and stains should be gone. In especially tough cases, you can repeat the same procedure and use a very fine 00 or 000 steel wool to work the acid solution in. This fine steel wool, combined with the acid cleaner, will pull off the water spots without scratching the glass.

Removing hard water marks is much slower than regular window cleaning. You should charge extra for this service.

NOTE: Any acid solution should be handled in a controlled way — it is advisable to wear heavy-duty rubber gloves. Before applying acid solution, cover the window ledge with a towel or drop cloth to prevent damage to this surface. Apply just enough to do the job and don't let it run down on to the sill. Avoid dripping it on floors, walls, furniture, etc. After cleaning, be sure to rinse and wipe the window frame as well as the glass to remove any residue. This is especially important when working on aluminum frame windows.

Acids can harm some types of soft glass, or specially-coated glass. **Read the product label for specifications and safety precautions.**

CLEANING VERY SMALL WINDOWS

Clean small panes just as you would any others. Use a smaller squeegee blade, 6" to 8". You can use a natural or synthetic sponge on panes that are too small for the strip washer. Or you can remove the sleeve from the strip washer handle and use the empty sleeve for washing smaller panes.

If you have a regular account where there are many small panes of the same size, you can cut a squeegee channel to the exact width of the panes by using a hack saw. (Smooth off the cut end with a file or emery paper to avoid scratching the window.)

In cleaning small panes, be sure to wipe the frames dry as you work down, or the water will drip down on the lower panes a few seconds after you have finished squeegeeing them.

NEW CONSTRUCTION WINDOW CLEANING

When you are cleaning new construction windows for the first time, they will usually have to be scraped to remove the debris from the construction work (paint, overspray, stucco, putty, stickers, etc.) To do the job right you will need a professional quality window scraper, 4" to 6" long.

Start by applying the window cleaning solution to the glass just as you would normally. To avoid scratching the window, hold the scraper at a slight angle to the glass and scrape in one direction only (not back and forth). Don't scrape too fast, and make sure the blade isn't getting dull. If the water begins to dry while you are scraping, apply more cleaning solution. **Never scrape a dry window.** When you have finished scraping the glass, rinse the window and clean again in the regular way.

IMPORTANT NOTE: On any new construction work be sure to inspect the windows in advance to see how bad they are, and to see if they have been scratched or defaced in any way during construction. If they have, this should be brought to the attention of the customer and noted in writing on your agreement or estimate with him **before you start the job.** You don't want the customer coming back later and claiming you scratched the glass.

On new construction work, you can figure your time will be at least two to three times what it would take to clean the same windows under ordinary conditions. Charge accordingly.

RESIDENTIAL WINDOW CLEANING

In residential work it isn't enough to get the windows clean. You have got to do neat, professional work to satisfy customers and get the referrals you want. When you finish a window be sure the sill is dry and there are no water spots on nearby furniture. If you have had to move knick knacks or furniture to get to the window, put them back just the way they were. (Do this immediately after you finish each window so that you don't forget.) Leave the area around the window just as you found it.

Residential window cleaning is a little slower than commercial work because of all the screens, sliding glass doors and other obstacles found in homes.

Screens — Screens will slow you down. Newer screens usually have springs on one side. You just press them one way and they pop out. Older ones may be more difficult to remove. When you cannot get an old screen off, you can sometimes take the sliding portion of the window out from the inside, lean it up against a wall, clean it on both sides and replace it. Place a towel behind the window so you don't scratch the wall and another one underneath to catch the drips.

Some customers will want the screens cleaned as well. Screens can be cleaned outside by using a horsehair counter brush, a damp towel or by hosing them down. Basically all you are trying to do is get the dust off them. If you hose the screens, do this first so they have time to dry while you are cleaning the glass.

Sliding glass doors — Clean sliding glass doors just like windows, but be sure to clean and wipe dry the rubber strip between the doors. Otherwise when you slide the door open it will streak the stationary door and you will have to start over.

RESIDENTIAL WINDOW CLEANING TIPS

1. When cleaning residential windows you need a drop cloth to protect the floor or window sills from the water running off the glass. Cut an ordinary towel in half the long way and sew the two halves together at the ends. This will form a long, narrow strip that you can put down in front of sliding glass doors, or you can double it up to fit most window sills without falling off.

2. For cleaning louvered windows use the Tricket (manufactured by Sorbo Products). This ingenious tool cleans both sides of the glass with one stroke.

3. Don't clean the rough opaque glass found in bathroom windows with your squeegee. It will wreck the sharp edge on your blade. Just wipe these windows quickly with a damp cloth. This will leave streaks, but no one can see them.

4. If you are working by yourself it is usually best to do the insides first. Then, when you clean the outside of the window, you will be able to tell if there are any spots you missed and which side they are on. It is easier to go back and touch up the insides than vice versa, especially in two-story homes.

5. Some homeowners will request that you clean the tracks on the sliding windows and doors. When you clean tracks be sure to do it before you wash the windows. You can use a toothbrush or similar tool, and a vacuum with a crevice attachment to get out all the loose dirt. Cleaning window tracks is not a part of regular window cleaning. Most window cleaners charge extra for this.

DEVELOPING A COMMERCIAL WINDOW CLEANING ROUTE

Success in commercial window cleaning comes by building a number of accounts into a concentrated route. For example, to clean a store with two large display windows and a glass door could take you 15 minutes. You may charge $8 to $10 for your service, but after you take into account your travel time and auto expense, it is hardly worth your while. However, if you have four accounts in that area of roughly the same size, your total work time would be about one hour and you would make $32 to $40 without increasing your travel and auto expense. Even if you charged just $5 per job, you could make $20 for the hour's work.

As soon as you get one account in an area, you should call on all the local businesses and try to line up more jobs to be done at the same time. Keep working on getting these accounts, using your local reference. This is the way to build a really profitable commercial window cleaning route.

How much you can charge a business account will depend somewhat on the area. In a major city where there is a lot of competition, you may be able to get just $5 for a small downtown shop, perhaps 15 to 20 minutes of work. For the same amount of work time at a store in an outlying, newer shopping area you may get $10 to $15.

SUBCONTRACTING WINDOW CLEANING WORK

If you do not want to clean windows yourself you can still include window cleaning service in your bids and subcontract the work out. This allows you to offer a more complete service to your customers. And you can make a nice additional profit on your janitorial accounts. Here are a few things to consider if you want to go the subcontracting route:

1. Make sure the window cleaner you choose is ready and willing to give you quick bids on the window portions of the jobs you are bidding on. You need to know how much he will charge you before you can include window cleaning in your proposal to the customer.

2. Go with a **window cleaning specialist** who does windows only. You'll get a professional job and you won't have to worry about the window cleaner stealing your account.

3. Find a subcontractor who shows up when the work is due and goes about his work in a professional manner. He will reflect on you and your company.

4. Be sure you work only with legitimate, insured subcontractors. (See Chapter 8)

5. Your subcontract relationship should be a mutually beneficial one. You are in a position to give the window cleaner a steady flow of work. He has contacts of his own and is in a position to steer janitorial accounts your way. Give him some of your business cards so he can refer you.

NOTE: For more information on the window cleaning business, (estimating, bidding, selling your service, etc.) get *The Professional Window Cleaning Manual, How To Make Money In Your Own Window Cleaning Business.* (See page 221)

Chapter 11
CARPET CLEANING

The five basic methods of modern carpet cleaning are rotary (or shampoo), dry foam, dry powder, bonnet cleaning and steam cleaning (or hot water extraction). Of these five methods, the first four are generally considered to be surface cleaning or **maintenance methods**, while the fifth method, steam cleaning, is considered to be a deep cleaning or **restorative method**.

Surface cleaning methods are frequently used by building maintenance contractors to keep carpet appearance at an acceptable level and to prolong the time between deep cleanings. It simply is not practical to bring in a steam cleaner every time you need to touch up a traffic lane or an entrance area.

Surface cleaning methods are commonly used when carpet drying time is a critical factor. Depending on the method you use, the carpet can be dry and ready for use almost immediately after cleaning.

ROTARY OR SHAMPOO METHOD

The rotary or shampoo method has been around for a long time. This is what old timers are referring to when they talk about "shampooing a rug".

Many contractors now consider rotary cleaning obsolete in comparison to modern techniques, because the shampooing process only spreads the soil around without removing much of it. Still, despite its limitations this method remains in wide use today, because it allows you to use one piece of equipment — the floor machine — for both carpet cleaning and hard floor care.

In rotary cleaning you use a regular floor machine equipped with a special nylon shower feed brush. A tank containing a shampoo solution is mounted on the handle of the floor machine. The operator controls the amount of shampoo flowing to the brush by a trigger near the machine handle. The actual cleaning process is similar to machine scrubbing a tile floor.

You start out by releasing a small amount of solution to the brush. Then you begin to move the floor machine slowly back and forth across the carpet, overlapping each stroke as you continue to release just enough solution to spread a thin layer of shampoo on the carpet. The action of the brush rotating over the carpet works the shampoo down into the carpet fibers and loosens and moves the soil around.

In large areas you should clean one section at a time, ten or twelve feet square, then move on section by section until the entire carpet is cleaned. Edges and areas that the machine cannot get to are done by hand with a scrub brush.

After the shampoo has dried, the carpet should be vacuumed with a regular upright vacuum or a pile lifter. The crystallized shampoo, along with some of the dirt, is picked up. The problem is that even after vacuuming, much of the shampoo residue remains in the carpet and actually continues to attract more dirt. This is why a shampooed carpet will often look dirtier a month or two after it is cleaned than it did before cleaning.

Shampooed carpets do look better right after cleaning because the soil has been spread around and the shampoo solution contains optical brighteners. But this is primarily a cosmetic form of cleaning. No dirt is removed by the floor machine and only a small amount comes out later in the vacuuming.

You can get somewhat better results by going over the carpet with a wet-dry vacuum right after the shampooing. This pulls out more of the dirty shampoo solution. But to do a really deep cleaning using the rotary method, you need to follow the shampooing with a thorough rinsing and extraction using a steam cleaning machine. In fact, the combination of rotary cleaning and steam cleaning is a very effective method of getting ground-in dirt and grime out of a badly soiled carpet. (See "Restoring Extremely Dirty Carpets", page 163.)

DRY FOAM METHOD

The dry foam method is a "gentle" method of cleaning carpets utilizing a foam rather than a liquid. The foam is generated from a concentrated shampoo inside the machine. This sudsy foam is then released onto a revolving cylindrical brush which works the suds into the carpet pile. After waiting an hour or two, the dirt-filled foam is vacuumed up with a regular upright vacuum. Some dry foam machines have a built-in vacuum which allows for one-pass cleaning.

Foam machines are fairly simple mechanically, and they require no great skill or experience to operate. Since no water is used there is little danger of overwetting, shrinkage and browning. And the carpet is dry and ready for use in a short period of time.

Like the rotary method the foam method leaves a certain amount of cleaning solution or residue in the carpet. When you foam clean an area on a regular basis, the residue gradually builds up and begins to attract dirt, requiring a periodic rinsing with an extraction machine.

Foam machines come in various sizes. The large units can clean up to 10,000 square feet per hour in one pass on large open areas. The combination of fast drying time, ease of use, safety and high production rates makes these machines very popular in large 24 hour accounts such as airports.

DRY POWDER METHOD

Dry powder cleaning is a surface cleaning method used extensively by many institutions and contractors. The main advantage of this method is that there is no waiting for the carpet to dry. As soon as the carpet is cleaned it is ready for immediate use. This makes dry cleaning especially useful in hotels, hospitals, restaurants, etc. where down time is really a problem. Since there is no water used there is zero danger of shrinkage and seam separation. Anyone can employ this method quickly and easily.

To dry clean carpets you need a dry cleaning compound, a special machine that has two counter-revolving brushes and a vacuum cleaner. The dry cleaning method consists of three steps:

1. Spread the powder (actually a moist compound containing solvents) by hand onto the area to be cleaned. Spread more in the traffic lanes and little or none along the edges.

2. Use the twin-brush machine to work the powder into the carpet. The two brushes revolving in opposite directions work the powder down, into and around the carpet fibers. As the solvent-laden powder is agitated and rubbed against the carpet fibers it begins to loosen and absorb the soil.

3. Vacuum up the dirt-saturated powder. The carpet is now ready for use.

The three steps make this a slower process than most other carpet cleaning methods. Dry powder cleaning is used by contractors as part of an ongoing maintenance program to keep carpet appearance at an acceptable level and prolong the time between deep cleanings.

BONNET CLEANING METHOD

Bonnet cleaning is a popular maintenance method with many contractors. You can use your floor machine and do a good job of surface cleaning without filling the carpet with shampoo. It is fast, easy and economical. Regular bonnet cleaning can greatly prolong the periods between deep cleanings.

To clean carpets using the bonnet method you need three things: a floor machine, some cleaning solution (such as Argo Sheen) and a specially constructed yarn bonnet. The bonnets come in a variety of styles and sizes, to fit just about any floor machine. For most types of commercial grade carpeting you want a bonnet with a tight short-looped construction. These hold up well and run smoothly across the carpeting. Floppy or fluffy bonnets tend to cause the machine to buck and wobble. The floor machine can be of any size but it should be the regular 175 RPM variety, not one of the high speed models.

To start cleaning, dip the bonnet right in the cleaning solution (in a mop pail) and wring it out. Mount the pad under the floor machine and simply run the machine back and forth on the carpet the same way you would if you were buffing a floor, overlapping each stroke.

As the damp bonnet moves across the carpet (under the weight of the floor machine) it wipes the surface soil off the carpet and onto the bonnet. When the pad gets dirty on one side you can turn it over and use the other side. Once the pad is completely saturated with dirt, you pull it off, rinse it out in clean water and dip it in the cleaning solution again. Then continue to clean.

Bonnet cleaning can be done as often as necessary without damaging the carpeting. For instance, you can touch up traffic lanes and entrance areas once a week if necessary. Bonnet cleaning leaves the carpet just slightly damp, not soaked, and the carpet usually will be dry in 30 minutes to an hour.

STEAM CLEANING

The term "steam cleaning" is actually a misnomer. The terminology that better describes the actual cleaning process is "hot water extraction". Carpets are not cleaned with steam but with hot water containing a chemical solution. The cleaning solution is sprayed into the carpet under pressure and continuously extracted with a high powered vacuum. The vacuum and spray apparatus are combined in a tool called a wand.

There are basically three types of steam cleaning equipment — portable, self-contained extractors and truck-mounted.

PORTABLE STEAM CLEANING

Portable steam cleaners, as the name implies, are smaller steam cleaning units that can be rolled about on wheels. This is the kind of steam cleaning equipment most people are familiar with — the kind you rent for do-it-yourself carpet cleaning.

Portable extractors have three basic parts: the machine itself, the hoses and the cleaning tool or wand. The machine consists of a solution tank, a recovery tank, a pressure pump and a vacuum motor. Two hoses run from the machine to the wand. One carries the pressurized cleaning solution and the other is a vacuum hose to carry the dirty water back to the recovery tank.

The wand can be a regular handheld wand (scrub wand) or a power head wand. The difference is that the power head wand has rotating or revolving brushes to provide greater agitation and deeper cleaning of the carpet fibers. The operator controls the flow of cleaning solution by pressing or releasing a trigger on the wand handle. The vacuum works continuously whether the solution is flowing or not.

SELF-CONTAINED EXTRACTORS

Self-contained extractors are a relatively new development in carpet cleaning. These units have no hoses. The wand or power head is incorporated into the machine itself. Some of the units operate on electricity while others operate off a battery, making them completely self-contained.

Self-contained extractors come in a range of sizes. The large, heavy-duty units resemble automatic scrubbers and can clean 12,000 square feet per hour in open areas. The small, lightweight models (50 to 100 pounds) look and operate more like large upright vacuums than the traditional steam cleaners.

Self-contained units are fast and easy to use. They may well be the wave of the future in portable steam cleaning equipment.

TRUCK-MOUNTED STEAM CLEANING

The truck-mounted units are similar in function to the portables except that the cleaning plant is permanently mounted in a vehicle rather than on wheels. Only the wand and the hoses go into the area to be cleaned. The wands are the same type as those used with the portable equipment and the actual cleaning method is similar, except that now you do not have to stop and move the machine back out of your way every few minutes! But this is where the similarity ends.

Truck-mounted steam cleaning plants are much larger and more powerful than the portables. They have much larger recovery tanks, more vacuum power (water lift), and more pump power (pounds per square inch or PSI). Consequently none of the portables, despite advertising claims, can pull as much dirt out of a carpet as the top of the line truck-mounts. When you combine the power of a truck-mounted cleaning plant and an experienced operator, you have today's state of the art carpet cleaning system.

Critics of this system say that the truck-mount is **too** powerful, that it damages carpeting. But usually the fault lies with inexperienced or careless operators rather than with the equipment. Truck-mounted steam cleaning requires more skill than any other method of carpet cleaning.

An inexperienced operator can easily overwet the carpet, causing shrinkage or seams to pull open. Modern wall-to-wall carpeting is stretched and overstretched when it is installed. When exposed to excessive water, it naturally starts to shrink. Too much water and it pulls away from the wall, requiring restretching or repair. Learning truck-mounted steam cleaning "on the job" by trial and error can prove costly!

STEAM CLEANING TECHNIQUE

Begin by mixing the correct amount of carpet cleaning chemical with water in the solution tank. After you turn the machine on, you start cleaning by depressing the trigger on the wand handle. Work the wand back and forth in a push-pull fashion. Be sure to overlap each stroke by a few inches. If you are using a regular scrub wand you will have to bear down a bit on the handle to properly agitate the carpet fibers. After several strokes release the trigger and go back over the area you have just cleaned with the vacuum only. This extra vacuuming helps to prevent overwetting the carpet. If you are cleaning correctly, most of the cleaning solution should remain in the carpet only momentarily.

When steam cleaning, you always start in the furthest area of the building or room and work your way backwards toward the exit or door. Take care not to clip furniture with the wand handle or bang the wand head into furniture legs or into the baseboards. Many carpet cleaners like to "cut out" a room by going along all the edges first, then cleaning the center.

If the carpet is very dirty, you can clean it a second time in the opposite direction (crossways to your first series of strokes). This second cleaning will often pull out as much dirt as your first pass. This is because the water and solution left in the carpet from the first cleaning have had longer to work and loosen the soil. Plus you are now cleaning different sides of the fiber. In extreme cases you can rotary clean the carpet first, then steam clean. (This method is described on page 163.)

When working with a power head wand the cleaning technique may be a little different, depending on the type of equipment you have. Some power heads have forward and rear spray nozzles and various types of brushes and other mechanisms designed to provide greater agitation and scrubbing of the carpet fibers. While these systems are a little more complex you will still be using the same basic back and forth overlapping cleaning stroke.

The one exception is the rotary power head (such as the popular RX-20 Rotary Jet System by Hydra-Master). This unit cleans in a side-to-side motion like a floor machine. When using this equipment you can first clean around the edges and corners with a regular scrub wand, then hook up the rotary power head and do the rest of the carpet, just as if you were buffing a hard floor. This is much easier and less tiring than the backward and forward strokes required with the regular scrub wand.

Steam cleaning is best accomplished with a team of two people. To do a thorough job it is necessary to move the furniture, clean underneath and put the furniture back. Your assistant can help you move the heavy pieces of furniture, and while you are cleaning, he or she can move the lighter pieces alone. If you are working with a portable steam cleaner, an assistant can also keep the machine and hoses back out of your way.

When you replace the furniture you should put carpet protectors (small foil-backed or plastic squares) under the furniture legs to prevent rust stains on the carpet. Small styrofoam blocks are available to keep large flat bottom objects like trunks or file cabinets up off the wet carpet.

If there are floor length curtains touching the carpet, they should be held up off the carpet until it dries. You can lay the ends of the curtains over a piece of furniture, or you can put them through a clothes hanger and hang them up on the curtain rod.

When you are finished cleaning, the last step is to quickly brush the carpet with a grooming brush to raise the nap. This speeds drying time and leaves the carpet with an even "finished" look. You can also speed drying time by leaving a fan or two blowing on the carpet, with as many windows open as possible.

SPOT CLEANING

No matter what type of carpet cleaning system you use, there will always be spots that require individual attention. On most commercial accounts, you will need to spot clean the carpet on a regular basis to keep it looking good.

Spot cleaning is a small science in itself. There are all sorts of elaborate spot cleaning procedures and charts telling exactly what to use on any given spot. Fortunately for the contract cleaner there are two spot cleaning solutions that will take out 95% of the spots you will run into. The two essential spotters you will need are a solvent (such as Ramsey's Volatile Dry Spotter) to take out the oil-based spots, and a general detergent spotter (such as Ramsey's General Spotter Concentrate) to take out the water-based spots.

The first step in spot cleaning is to try and determine if the spot is water-based (proteins, milk, sodas, chocolate, etc.) or oil-based (tar, grease, asphalt, etc.) If the spot smells or feels oily, use the volatile dry spotter. Pour a little bit on a clean towel and rub the spot gently. If the spot is oil-based it will start to dissolve immediately into the cloth, and you will notice that the cloth is picking up the color of the spot. Continue to clean by applying more solvent and rubbing until all of the spot is transferred from the carpet to the cloth. As you clean, use different areas of the cloth so you do not wipe the oil back into the rug.

If the spot appears to be a water-based spot, use the detergent spotter. Pour some out on a cloth or towel and dab or gently rub in a circular direction. Don't scrub hard as this can distort the carpet pile. Next, wipe the spot with a dry part of the towel. Continue by alternately dabbing with the solution and drying with the towel until all of the stain is picked up.

If you cannot tell whether the spot is oil or water-based, use the solvent first. Then if the solvent does little or nothing to move the spot, try the detergent spotter. It is best to wait a few minutes to allow the solvent time to dry.

Coffee stains are one of the most common stains you will run into on your commercial accounts. These will usually come up with the general spotter. If not, you can try Tannin Stain Remover. This product also works well on tea, liquor and some juice stains.

If you find a spot before it has dried you will have a much better chance of getting it out without leaving a stain. But you must take care not to spread the spot — always work from the outer edges of the spill toward the center, to avoid spreading the spot further.

Do not scrub a spot briskly with a brush. This can distort the carpet pile and leave you with a worse problem than you started out with. If the spot is going to come out at all it will be the action of the chemicals that will move it, rather than your elbow grease.

If you are going to be doing much carpet cleaning you should invest in a good spotting kit and learn how to use it. An excellent kit is the Ramsey Master

Spotting Kit. It contains ten spotting agents, a spot cleaning chart and several useful hand tools in a handy caddy.

In addition to this kit, you will need chewing gum remover. You just spray it on the gum. The gum freezes and you can chip it off easily with a scraper tool.

Another useful spot cleaning tool is the Amway handheld rug shampoo applicator. Although designed mainly for home use, this inexpensive tool comes in handy for quickly touching up all kinds of spots in your commercial accounts. You just work the shampooer gently over the area to be cleaned, then dry with a towel.

NOTE: Before applying any high-powered commercial spotters it is a good idea to test the carpet for color fastness or possible discoloration. To do this take a cloth and rub a little of the cleaning solution into the carpet (in an out-of-the-way area). Watch to see if any of the carpet colors bleed or transfer onto the cloth.

MAINTAINING AND CLEANING TRAFFIC LANE AREAS

Maintaining the traffic lane areas is one of the biggest cleaning challenges you will face in your commercial accounts. This is where most of the really heavy build-up of soil will be. And these are also the most highly visible areas.

Maintaining traffic areas starts with prevention — keeping as much dirt out of the building and the traffic lanes as possible. Walk-off mats should go at all the entrances, especially the doorways off the parking areas. The bigger and longer the mats the better. Commercial grade mats can be purchased at a janitorial supply store, or the building owner can make arrangements with a mat service.

Traffic areas should be thoroughly vacuumed every time you clean the account. Use a heavy duty commercial upright vacuum. (Vacuums without beater bars will not get as much of the ground-in dirt out of these high use areas.)

As time goes by the traffic lanes become soiled and it will take more than vacuuming to get them clean. Now you must go to one of the surface methods of carpet cleaning — bonnet, rotary, dry foam or dry powder. If you employ the bonnet method you can use your floor machine to remove the surface soil without filling the carpet with shampoo.

Eventually, depending on the building, the traffic areas may deteriorate to the point that you will not be able to keep them looking good with any of the surface cleaning methods. Now you need to use the restorative method of carpet cleaning — steam cleaning. You can steam clean just the traffic areas or the whole carpet.

When you steam clean you should first "pre-spray" the traffic lane areas. Use a traffic lane cleaner, like Pre-Oil Break, in a pump-up type pressure sprayer. Spray the traffic lanes and other heavily soiled areas a few minutes before starting to steam clean. You want the traffic lane cleaner to have time to chemically break down the heavy accumulation of grease and dirt ground into the traffic lanes. Then, when the hot water spray and vacuum from the wand pass over these areas they will blast out and remove the loosened soil.

RESTORING EXTREMELY DIRTY CARPETS

If you have an extremely dirty carpet or traffic lane, you can often get it to come clean using a three-step process:

1. **Pile lift** — Go over the entire carpet with a pile lifter. This will remove most of the loose dry soil. (Use a commercial upright if you don't have a pile lifter.)

2. **Rotary scrub** — Thoroughly scrub a section of the carpet with a rotary floor machine equipped with a shower feed nylon brush. The aggressive action of the nylon brush turning under the weight of the machine works the cleaning solution deep down into and around all the carpet fibers.

3. **Rinse and extraction** — After the scrubbed-in shampoo has had a little time to work on the dirt, follow with a complete rinsing using a steam extractor, preferably a truck-mount. The steam cleaning process flushes out and removes all the shampoo and emulsified soil.

Do the whole carpet section by section. Don't rotary scrub too large an area at once, or the shampoo will start to dry before you are able to rinse it out. This three-step procedure is time-consuming, but it is one way to restore life to an extremely dirty carpet that has been given up for dead by other cleaners.

CLEANING STAIN RESISTANT CARPETING

Stain resistant nylon carpeting is manufactured using a special process which produces a high degree of stain resistance in the carpet fiber itself. This new generation of carpeting requires special cleaning methods — carpet manufacturers have warned that using cleaning methods and chemicals not compatible with stain resistant carpeting can impair the stain resistant nature of the carpeting and void their warranty.

Most manufacturers agree that hot water extraction is an effective method for cleaning this new type of carpeting. Here are some basic guidelines for the safe cleaning of stain resistant carpeting:

1. Use only those cleaning chemicals designed specifically for stain resistant carpets. (Cleaning solutions should be anionic and have a PH of less than 10.) Ask your supplier for recommendations.

2. Do not use more than the recommended amount of cleaning chemical. Using too much detergent leaves a residue in the carpet which may affect the stain resistance.

3. Water temperature should not be greater than 130 degrees Fahrenheit. If you are not sure how hot the water you are using is, use **warm water** only.

4. First clean the carpet overall. Then spot clean only if necessary. Avoid overwetting and heavy duty scrubbing.

5. If you use any type of topical treatment (soil retardant), make sure it is one that is recommended for the type of stain resistant carpeting you are cleaning.

LEARNING THE TRADE

Ideally you should learn the ropes by working with an experienced carpet cleaner before setting out on your own. The cleaning of carpet fabrics is a technical field and the real professionals in the trade are known as carpet cleaning technicians.

On your way to becoming a qualified "tech" there is much to be learned. You must be able to identify a wide range of carpets and their cleaning characteristics. You need to know how different types of cleaning chemicals and water temperatures affect carpet fabrics. You need to know how to mix chemicals; how to identify and remove all sorts of spots and stains; how to recognize potential problems in carpet installation and seams; and how to make minor (and sometimes major) carpet repairs. Plus you will need to learn how to work with and get the most out of the equipment you employ. You do not need to be a chemist or an engineer to clean carpets, but a little mechanical aptitude sure comes in handy.

Carpet cleaning is a rapidly changing field. New types of carpeting are coming on the market all the time. Some of these fabrics require new cleaning methods. For example, when the carpets with built-in stain resistance first came out, many carpet cleaners did not know how to safely clean them. There is always more to learn. (See "Carpet Cleaning Information" in the Resources chapter.)

WHAT KIND OF CARPET CLEANING SYSTEM IS RIGHT FOR YOU?

The cleaning contractor looking to buy his first carpet cleaning system is confronted with a bewildering variety of carpet cleaning machines and methods — dry cleaning, foam extractors, steam cleaners, hot and cold water extractors, spin bonnet systems, shampooers, single disk rotary scrubbers, etc.

To make things more confusing, all the manufacturers tout their products and methods with advertising phrases like "deepest", "fastest", "best", etc. With all the contradictory advertising claims it is easy to be overwhelmed, but don't be. If you want to get into carpet cleaning all you need to do is evaluate your needs, do a little comparative shopping and **pick a system that works for you** — one that you can afford and that does the job you want it to do.

There really is no "best" method of carpet cleaning. Each method has its place. It all depends on the kind of carpet cleaning required. For instance, if you do mainly janitorial work, your first concern will be to keep the carpets in your accounts looking good on a regular, ongoing basis. You will need to vacuum and spot clean regularly, and use one of the surface cleaning methods periodically to keep the carpet appearance at a satisfactory level. (You can use the foam, dry powder or rotary shampoo methods, or you can simply buy a few spin bonnets and use your floor machine.) When the time comes to steam clean the carpets you can always subcontract the job out. Then later as your business grows, you can purchase a portable extractor and maybe eventually a truck-mount.

On the other hand if you are primarily in the carpet cleaning business your customers will expect a deep cleaning, not just a touch-up or surface cleaning. For this purpose you will need steam cleaning equipment. You can always start out with the portable units. They are much cheaper than the truck mounts and do an acceptable job. Lots of carpet cleaning companies are using them and doing a good business. However, these days more and more homeowners and businesses are expecting and requesting truck-mounted steam cleaning.

No matter what kind of equipment you buy, getting into carpet cleaning on a professional level requires a substantial investment. Prices range from a few hundred dollars for a used floor machine and some spin bonnets to $20,000 or more for a deluxe truck-mount set up. Although the full price of a new piece of carpet cleaning equipment may seem prohibitive, it is usually possible to make a small down payment and purchase the machine on a lease plan. That way the machine can pay for itself as you make money cleaning carpets.

Many manufacturers and some distributors provide classes, training and ongoing support for the equipment they sell. You should take this into consideration when deciding which carpet cleaning system to purchase.

CARPET CLEANING SUPPLIES AND ACCESSORIES

The kind of supplies and carpet cleaning accessories you need will depend largely on the kind of carpet cleaning equipment you own. Most janitorial supply stores also carry carpet cleaning supplies. Here is a quick overview of some of the basic supplies and accessories used in the carpet cleaning business:

Spot cleaning kit — An excellent kit is the Ramsey Master Spotting Kit. It contains ten spotting agents — General Spotter, Traffic Lane Cleaner, Volatile Dry Spotter, Tannin Stain Remover, Spotting Shampoo, Pre-Oil Break, Kil-Odor, Rust Remover, Paint, Oil & Grease Remover and Pre-Upholstery Conditioner. Also included is a bone scraper, a spotting brush and a spotting chart. Costs about $75 and well worth it.

Measuring wheel — Used to quickly measure the size of a room, house or building when you are giving a carpet cleaning estimate based on square feet. Cost is around $25 to $50.

Knee kicker — A carpet installer's tool used by carpet cleaners to restretch a carpet back on to the tack strip. Hopefully not needed too often. Costs about $50 to $75.

Carpet brush or groomer — Used at the completion of a job to fluff up the carpeting. Helps speed drying time and gives the carpet a nice, uniform appearance. Cost is about $20.

Pile lifter — A large, super heavy-duty vacuum that really knocks loose dirt out of the carpet. Cost is $800 to $1,000. Look for used ones.

Carpet protectors (coasters) — For keeping furniture off the carpet while it dries. The foil-backed or plastic squares cost about $40 for a case of 5,000. The styrofoam blocks cost about $40 for a case of 1,000.

Air movers — Specially shaped fans that keep the air circulating over the carpet. Greatly speed drying time. Cost around $200.

Pressure sprayers — Handheld pump-up type sprayers used to pre-spray spots and traffic lanes and to apply carpet treatments, such as soil retardants. Cost is around $50.

Defoamer — A chemical used in steam extractors to neutralize the foam that clogs up the vacuum hoses. The foam is created by shampoos left in the carpet from previous surface cleaning methods. Cost is $3 a gallon.

Bone scraper — Used in spot cleaning to work cleaning solution into the carpet without damaging the fibers. Costs about $5.

Upholstery and stair cleaning tools — Small handheld wands for cleaning stairs, upholstery and hard-to-get-at places.

Gum remover — A spray that freezes gum so that you can chip it off with a bone scraper. Comes in an aerosol can. Approximate cost is $2.50 for a 12 oz. can.

Power head wands — For steam cleaning machines. They come in a wide variety of shapes and sizes. Designed to agitate, scrub or separate the carpet fibers so that the chemical spray can penetrate and clean more thoroughly. Built-in vacuum extracts the loosened soil. Usually less fatiguing to operate then the regular scrub wand.

Anti-static treatment — Helps to eliminate static electricity. Usually applied after cleaning.

Optical brighteners — Included in carpet cleaning solutions to bring out the colors in the carpeting. A cosmetic product that makes carpets appear clean and bright.

Deodorizers — Chemicals put in the carpet cleaning solution or sprayed on the carpet to neutralize odors.

Soil retardants — For example, "Scotchgard". Applied on a freshly cleaned carpet to slow the resoiling process. Sometimes included in the carpet cleaning solution.

Steam cleaning chemicals — Come in either concentrated powder or liquid form for mixing with water in the solution tank. May contain optical brighteners, deodorants, defoamers, solubilizers, emulsifiers, soil retardants, anti-static agents or solvents. Specially formulated detergents are available for the new stain resistant type of carpeting.

Chapter 12
FLOOR MAINTENANCE

In the last ten years new technology has completely changed the way hard floors are cared for. New and better floor finish products have made the old style waxes obsolete for most types of floors. Ultra high speed floor machines and machineless-rinseless strippers have made many floor care operations faster, easier and less expensive.

Floor maintenance is a specialized and increasingly technical field. There is a great deal to learn and mistakes can be costly. In the beginning, take on only those floor care jobs you can handle. Hire experienced floor care people to take care of situations you are not familiar with, or subcontract the work out.

This chapter will give you a basic introduction to the equipment and methods used in modern floor maintenance. If you want more technical information the trade magazines are full of detailed articles. (See the Resources chapter.)

FLOOR MAINTENANCE EQUIPMENT

The floor machine is the central piece of equipment in most floor maintenance programs. There are two basic types of floor machines — the conventional floor machines or "buffers" and the newer high speed machines or "burnishers".

The conventional floor machine and conventional floor care methods are discussed below. The high speed machines and methods are covered later in this chapter under "High Speed Floor Maintenance".

THE CONVENTIONAL FLOOR MACHINE (BUFFER) has been around for decades. This is the basic "buffer" most people are familiar with. A conventional floor machine operates at about 175 RPM's (revolutions per minute). On floor machines the RPM is a measurement of pad or brush speed.

Floor machines are measured by the width of the pad or brush they utilize. The larger the machine the faster it will accomplish its work. A machine in the 16" to 20" range is suitable for all-around floor care. New 20" machines start at about $500 and go up from there, depending on the features you want. Fortunately, because of their sturdy construction and long life, there are always good used machines available.

The conventional floor machine is quite versatile and, with a variety of brushes and pads, may be used for stripping, buffing, scrubbing, spray buffing, baseboard cleaning, carpet shampooing and bonnet cleaning.

FLOOR MACHINE BRUSHES are made of a variety of fibers. Stiffer bristles are used for stripping and scrubbing. Softer fibers are used for polishing.

Brushes can be attached to the machine only when it is turned **off**. Tip the machine back and place the brush over the circular drive mechanism underneath the machine. Now rotate the brush to the left (counterclockwise) as far as it will go. This locks the brush in place. To remove the brush simply turn it sharply back to the right (clockwise).

Never leave the machine standing or sitting on the brush for long. This distorts and eventually ruins the brush fibers.

FLOOR PADS — Synthetic floor pads are preferred over brushes by many contractors. Pads are color coded to indicate their degree of abrasiveness. The finer buffing pads are a light shade while the heavy-duty stripping pads are darker colors and black. The very fine pads for conventional buffing are white.

The pads are generally placed on the floor under a drive pad. The drive pad is constructed like a brush, only instead of having fibers, it has a tufted or bristled surface to grab and hold a floor pad. It is attached to the machine in the same way as a brush. The floor pad is simply laid on the floor and the machine is tipped back, rolled directly over, centered and set down on the pad.

Pads should always be rinsed out and hung up to dry after each use. If they are very dirty, they can be cleaned by soaking in a solution of stripper and water overnight, then rinsed out. Old floor pads may be cut up for use in hand-scrubbing operations.

Steel wool pads are the old standby, still in use by some contractors. They should not be used on terrazzo or marble floors, however, as small particles of steel may become imbedded in the floor, causing rust stains.

WET-DRY VACUUMS are used primarily for picking up dirty water, cleaning solution and rinse water, following floor stripping and scrubbing operations. This is much faster, easier and more efficient than using a mop. These machines can also be used for normal carpet vacuuming in places where there are too many obstacles for an upright vacuum.

Wet-dry vacuums are equipped with a long hose which makes them ideal for vacuuming hard-to-get-at spots, high places and draperies. They are also used in some carpet cleaning operations to pick up shampoo after rotary scrubbing.

Tank capacity ranges anywhere from three to fifty gallons. A machine with a five to ten gallon capacity is adequate for most day-to-day maintenance operations. The unit should be on large wheels for easy transport. In choosing a wet-dry vacuum, be sure to find a model that can be emptied easily. New five gallon machines start at about $300; ten gallon machines at $400.

AUTOMATIC SCRUBBERS are large walk-behind or rider machines that combine two rotary scrubbing brushes, a large floor squeegee and a powerful wet-dry vacuum for large area floor scrubbing or stripping. The machine does the work of two men, one scrubbing and the other operating a wet-dry vacuum.

Automatic scrubbers save a tremendous amount of time and labor but they are also expensive. You need to have a major hard floor account to justify the purchase of an automatic scrubbing machine. These machines are used primarily in large accounts such as supermarkets, factories or department stores.

HAND TOOLS AND ACCESSORIES

Straw broom — Standard kitchen broom. Get a good quality one or it will leave more straw on the floor than the dirt you pick up. Used in small or congested areas.

Whisk broom — Used for sweeping crevices and edges.

Counter brush — A small horsehair broom used mainly for sweeping litter into a dust pan.

Push brooms — Normally used on large areas. They come in a range of fiber stiffness, depending on the surface to be swept. Soft horsehair brooms, 18" to 36", are useful for sweeping inside hard surface areas (offices, lunchrooms, storerooms, etc.)

Wet mops — Mops for professional use come in a range of sizes from 12 ounces to 32 ounces. A larger person will generally use a heavier mop. Mopheads are replaceable and attach to the handle in a variety of ways. A small nylon scrubbing pad can be attached to the mophead to provide scrubbing power to remove black marks and heavy soil. Regular laundering of mopheads will increase their life.

Buckets and wringers — Come in all shapes and sizes. A good all-around unit is an oval pail on wheels, with downward pressure wringer.

Doodlepad scrubber — This useful tool is a scrub pad holder with a swivel on an extension handle. Allows you to detail scrub or strip floor edges, corners and baseboards without stooping over.

Dust mops — The fastest way to pick up loose dirt from hard surface floors. Comes in sizes from 12" to 72".

Dust pan — Get the heavy-duty metal ones, for professional use.

Lamb's wool wax applicator — For applying smooth, even coats of finish on all types of floors.

Floor squeegee — Used in floor stripping and scrubbing operations for drying floors and helping to pick up stripping solution, etc.

Floor scraper or putty knife — For quickly removing foreign substances from hard surface floors.

Hand scrub pads — Nylon scrubbing pads used for detailing small, hard-to-get-at floor and baseboard areas.

Baseboard brushes — For cleaning wax build-up off baseboards. Power-operated baseboard brushes are now available.

Caution signs — "Wet Floor" signs for keeping people off your working area. May be cones, signs or barricades.

FLOOR CARE PRODUCTS

When purchasing floor care products the importance of cultivating a good working relationship with your local janitorial supply dealer cannot be overstated. The first thing to do is locate a knowledgeable supplier that you can trust. Buy all of your floor care products from him and he will be glad to help you get the right supplies for your jobs. If you have a special cleaning problem, he will either have the answer or know where to get it.

It is a good idea to purchase floor care products in small quantities in the beginning, until you have discovered which products work best for you. There is an almost endless array of floor finishes, sealers and strippers on the market today. While some of the advertising claims made about these products are exaggerated, there are excellent ones available.

Good quality is a smart investment. Remember that the products you use are directly related to the time and energy required to do the job. The direct expense of floor care supplies in any floor maintenance operation is small compared to the overall budget. Labor costs are always your biggest expense. You may save a few dollars on a gallon of floor finish, but if the floor needs frequent recoating or takes twice as much work to maintain, you are losing money.

Because of the one-to-one relationship between time and money in this business, a few minutes saved here and there can make a big difference in profit.

FLOOR FINISH — Floor finishes (waxes, polishes, etc.) serve both to protect and enhance the appearance of a hard floor surface. Volumes have been written on the chemical properties and formulas of thousands of different floor coatings. Without getting technical, finishes for conventional floor care may be divided into three basic categories — fully buffable, non-buffable and semi-buffable.

Fully buffable finishes are "soft" floor waxes. They work well in traffic areas that receive a lot of abrasion from loose soil or sand. When the wax gets dulled and marred, its shine can be quickly restored by dry buffing.

Non-buffable finishes are harder floor polishes that show little if any improvement from dry buffing, but on more lightly traveled floors will require less maintenance than the buffable type. These harder finishes are usually maintained by spray buffing.

Non-buffable finishes dry to a high luster and stay bright, tending to scratch rather than dull, as the softer waxes do. This makes them more suitable for use on residential floors, where regular buffing is impractical, or in commercial applications where a regular spray buffing program is employed.

Semi-buffable finishes — Many of the finishes used in conventional floor maintenance share some of the qualities of both the buffable and non-buffable finishes. These products dry to a reasonable shine and still respond fairly well to dry buffing.

When you find a floor finish that works for you, stay with it. In order to change from one floor finish system to another you must strip it all down and start from scratch. The labor and expense involved may not justify your experiment. Of course, if your present floor care system is unsatisfactory you have little choice but to change.

Consider the type of floor, the traffic conditions and how much time you can afford to spend on maintenance. Choose a good quality floor finish that is suited to the circumstances. This is where the advice of a good supplier can really help you.

FLOOR SEALER — Sealers are used to seal the surface of porous floors prior to waxing. Many of the new floor coverings as well as the very hard surfaces do not require sealing.

In selecting a sealer, be sure to get a type that is compatible with both the floor surface and the finish you intend to use. Ask your supplier for advice.

FLOOR STRIPPER — Stripping solutions are used to dissolve old coats of floor finish from hard surface floors. There are all-purpose strippers and stripping solutions formulated specifically to remove certain types of finishes or waxes. Solutions containing solvents are used for stripping wood floors.

Floor finish products usually have instructions on the label as to which and how much stripping solution to use. The right stripping solution combined with the scrubbing power of a floor machine will strip almost any finish.

New machineless-rinseless strippers have been developed. These products strip floors without the need for a machine or for rinsing after stripping. Hard as it may be for many veterans in the business to accept, these new strippers do work well in many situations. (See "Machineless Stripping" and "Machineless-Rinseless Stripping" later in this chapter)

SPRAY BUFF SOLUTION — This product is used with a floor machine in spray buffing floors. You can purchase it in a liquid or spray form from your janitorial supplier, or you can mix your own using a solution of one half water and one half floor finish (the same type as the base coat).

NOTE: In spray buffing with high speed equipment, use only those products specifically designed for the type of high speed finish you are using. (See "High Speed Floor Maintenance")

NEUTRALIZING SOLUTION can be used in the rinse water (after stripping) to neutralize the alkali residue left over from the stripping solution. If not removed, this stripper residue can cause problems with the floor finish.

DEGREASER — An expensive detergent which cuts through grease. Essential if you are doing any restaurant or industrial floor maintenance. Should be highly concentrated.

DUST MOP TREATMENTS come in liquid or spray, either wax or oil base. These are used to treat or "cure" dust mops, causing the dust to cling to the mophead. Using too much will leave streaks on the floor. Wax treatments are preferable to oil base treatments on most types of floors.

PRODUCT SAFETY NOTES

1. **Always carefully follow directions on the label** of any product you use.
2. **Do not experiment** — Seek competent help from suppliers, experienced contractors, manufacturers' agents, etc.
3. **Do not mix chemicals**, especially bleach and ammonia. These combine to produce a poisonous gas. Even allowing the fumes to mix in an enclosed room can do you in.

FLOOR MAINTENANCE TECHNIQUES

DUST MOPPING

Dust mopping is the fastest way to remove loose dirt from smooth, hard floor surfaces. You can mop a thousand square feet in five to ten minutes, depending on the congestion. The main points to remember are:

1. Don't lift the mop off the floor unless you are making a pile.
2. Keep the same edge forward until you are ready to shake out the dirt into a pile.
3. Avoid bumping the mop against chair legs and corners, or you will leave a deposit of dirt there.
4. Use a larger mop whenever possible.
5. Wash and retreat mopheads regularly. Do not use too much treatment solution.

SWEEPING

Choose the right kind of broom for the job. If you have a rough or wet surface, use a push broom. Push brooms with coarse bristles (street brooms) are used for heavy duty sweeping and outside work. Soft horsehair bristles are used for finer sweeping on interior floors.

In areas of heavy obstruction such as a kitchen, you can use a corn broom or counter brush. First go around the room and sweep the debris out from under the tables, desks, ovens, etc. Then come down the main open areas with the push broom.

MOPPING

The most important thing to remember about mopping is the sweeping. If the floor has not been properly swept, mopping will not get it clean.

It is surprising how few people know how to mop a floor correctly. Pushing a mop back and forth like a vacuum cleaner is highly inefficient and fatiguing. The proper technique is to walk backwards with the mop, while swinging it from side to side in long, slender figure eights, or overlappings S's.

As you work, try to keep your back straight. This will keep you from tiring too quickly. Mopping, when correctly performed, is actually fairly easy work. Choose the mopping operation that best suits the job at hand:

Spot mopping — Cleaning only those areas of a floor that are soiled.

Damp mopping — Cleaning an entire area with a well wrung-out mop, to remove minor soil and dust. When damp mopping a highly polished floor, use warm or cold water only. (Hot water can dull the finish.)

Wet mopping — Spread a cleaning solution across a heavily soiled floor. Let the detergent remain on the floor for a few minutes, then scrub with the mop. The solution can be picked up with a well wrung-out mop. Rinse the floor, if required.

It is an efficient practice to "cut out" an area before you mop it entirely. This means quickly mopping along beside the baseboards before mopping the adjacent open area. This should be done with a wrung-out mop to avoid slopping the cleaning solution on the wall or baseboard.

The commonly used mophead weighs about 24 ounces, but you should choose a weight that suits your body size and strength. Be sure to clean, rinse, wring out and hang up wet mops after use. If you pour your dirty mop water into a sink, be sure you rinse it all away.

NOTE: When using any kind of tool with a long handle, be sure to remember both ends — the end that cleans and the other end, the one that breaks windows, knocks things off desks and puts holes in plasterboard.

OPERATING A FLOOR MACHINE

Conventional floor machines (buffers or floor polishers) do their job by moving from side to side. This is usually accomplished by squeezing the handle and moving it up and down. Some of them have a hair trigger. When first learning to operate one, you may feel that you've got a bull by the horns. After putting a six-inch crease in your refrigerator door and taking a leg off your kitchen table, you begin to develop a respect for the beast!

The only way to learn is by practising. Just make sure you've got a big enough area to practise in. The trick lies in not over-reacting when the machine goes left or right. On a machine that rotates counterclockwise, a slight upward pull on the handle will send it to the right and a slight push down will take it back to the left. Each machine is a little different though, so you will have to get the feel of your own.

Actually, it's easy. In a few minutes you'll get the hang of it. Once you learn you will be able to control it effortlessly. Always maintain a respect for the machine though. If you get overconfident and careless, it is easy to break things.

DRY BUFFING

Dry buffing is used to restore the shine to a dulled waxed floor. It is most effective when a buffable wax has been used. Dry buffing is the easiest maintenance operation you can perform with a floor machine.

Use the soft brush or buffing pad and move the machine back and forth across the floor, slightly overlapping each stroke. Always keep the cord behind you so you don't run over it. (You could try putting it over your shoulder.)

Once you've got the hang of the basic technique, try tipping the machine up on one side a little. Push down on one handle and pull up on the other. This puts a great deal of weight on one edge of the buffer. This maneuver is called **heeling** the machine and is used to apply extra scrubbing power to an especially tough mark on the floor.

SPRAY BUFFING

Conventional spray buffing is both a polishing and a cleaning technique. By spray buffing a floor you can remove soil and black marks and produce a high gloss shine.

In this method you use a trigger spray bottle filled with spray buff solution. Spray about 15 to 20 square feet of floor in front of you with a light mist. Buff the area with a buffing pad until the floor is dry and shining. The floor appears dull at first, but comes to a high gloss as you continue to buff. This should remove the scuffs and soil as well. If not, spray again and heel the machine on the bad places. If spray buffing is done correctly, it should greatly extend the length of time between stripping operations.

Both dry and spray buffing create dust, so you will need to use a dust mop after these operations to ensure a really finished look to the floor.

MACHINE SCRUBBING

Eventually a floor gets to a condition where no amount of mopping or buffing can make it come clean. Now it is time to machine scrub and refinish. To do the job efficiently you will need at least two mops and two buckets with wringers. A wet-dry vacuum will save you a lot of time.

Both scrubbing and stripping are most easily done in two-man crews. The first step is to clear the area to be cleaned of all obstacles. Then spread a mild detergent solution **evenly and not too heavily** over the floor. Follow dilution instructions for the particular detergent you use. You don't want too strong a mixture or it might start to strip the floor.

Don't flood the floor or slop the solution on walls or furniture. If you are working by yourself, only lay solution on about 100 square feet of floor (10' x 10') at a time.

Now place a scrubbing pad under the floor machine and start scrubbing the floor from the far wall working backwards toward the door. Heel the machine on the bad areas. If you've got a partner working with you, he or she can start to pick up the cleaning solution from the scrubbed areas while you continue scrubbing. The solution can be picked up with either a damp wrung-out mop or a wet-dry vacuum, which is much easier.

If you have no partner, you will have to stop after doing about 100 square feet and pick up yourself. The all-important thing is not to let the detergent solution stand on the floor too long. **This cannot be overemphasized.** If the water remains too long it may seep through and cause the floor tiles to buckle, or the corners may start to rise up. Be especially careful of overwetting the "place and stick" tile often found in homes.

Once the floor is scrubbed, go back and rinse it. This must be done with a clean mop and clean water. You can either damp mop it dry or use the wet-dry vacuum. The vacuum will dry it almost instantly, whereas you will have to wait a few minutes after damp mopping.

Once you are sure the floor is dry you can apply one or two thin coats of floor finish. Use a clean mop or wax applicator for this. If you use a mop, get it wet first and wring it out completely before placing it in the finish. This prevents the mop from soaking up too much of the expensive finish.

You must exercise great caution when moving around on wet floor surfaces. They are slippery, and you should wear a shoe or boot which gives you some traction. Use even greater caution in making sure that no one else comes walking across the floor. If there is the slightest possibility of this happening, put out caution signs ("Wet Floor") to warn them, or rope off the area.

MACHINE STRIPPING

When even scrubbing isn't enough to restore a floor, you will have to resort to stripping. Stripping a floor should be done as infrequently as possible because it is a major operation, involving considerable time and sweat. However, when wax builds up and the floor is hopelessly marked, you will have to strip it down and start over again. Both scrubbing and stripping are tricky and you should learn **on the job** from someone who has the know-how before you attempt it yourself.

Before starting, clear the area and make sure you have all the necessary tools and supplies lined up and ready to go. You will need:

1. A floor machine with a black stripping pad.
2. A stripping solution.
3. A wet-dry vacuum.
4. Three mops and three mop buckets with wringers — one with stripper solution, one for finish and one with rinse water and neutralizer.
5. A brush or pad for stripping the edges.
6. Some clean towels.
7. Wet floor signs (optional).

If there are doorways leading off the area to be stripped, put down towels to keep the stripping solution from running on to another floor area you don't want to strip. Dilute and spread the stripping solution, following the instructions on the label to the letter. Put out stripper on just a small area at a time, no more than 10' by 10'.

Let the stripper sit and work on the floor for a few minutes. (See the product label for the recommended time.) Now use the floor machine in the same way as in scrubbing. Have your partner pick up the stripping solution with a wet-dry vacuum after you've gone by. If this solution, known as "slurry", is allowed to dry, it will not come off with a mop and you'll have to rewet the floor with stripping solution and scrub again. This is where a wet-dry vacuum really pays for itself.

In addition to cleaning the main floor area, you will have to hand strip all along the edges, corners and baseboards. These areas usually have the most wax build-up. Do this hand stripping while you are letting the stripping solution work on the floor. Use a doodle pad, hand pad or a baseboard brush. Another way to strip the edges is with a nylon scrubbing pad attached to the mophead.

After removing the stripper with the wet-dry vacuum, the floor should be rinsed with a neutralizing solution in water and the water picked up. Then rinse the floor again with clear water and damp mop dry.

After the floor is dry, you can apply two or three coats of finish. Several thin coats make for a more attractive, durable finish than one heavy one. Allow each coat of finish to dry before applying the next. Apply the finish very thinly and sparingly along the edges, to avoid creating a build-up along the baseboards and in the corners. It is this yellow build-up that often causes you to have to strip the floor in the first place! If you are putting two coats of finish on the floor, let only the second coat come right up to the edge.

If the floor is completely stripped down, you may need to apply a coat of sealer as your first coat. Some floors do not require sealing, however. (See "Types of Floors" later in this chapter.) Always use a clean mop or lamb's wool applicator and spread the finish or sealer evenly. Don't saturate the wax applicator or mop. Leave doors and windows open if possible to speed the drying time, but keep people and animals off.

MACHINELESS STRIPPING

In the last few years new stripping solutions have been developed that require no machine scrubbing. These products are called "no-scrub" strippers, "no machine" strippers or "machineless" strippers.

When using a machineless stripper you first clear the floor and place towels at the doorways, as you would in machine stripping. Next, dilute the no-scrub stripper in water according to the manufacturers' directions on the label. The amount of stripping solution you use will depend on the condition of the floor. It is a good idea to test a little of the diluted stripper on a small section of the floor to see if it will do the job. If not, add more stripper.

When you have determined the correct dilution, apply the stripping solution to a manageable portion of the floor with a mop. Let the stripper sit for the time specified by the manufacturer, usually not more than five minutes. Depending on the product used you may also need to agitate the solution with the mop. You will usually do this after allowing the stripper to soak for a few minutes. Be sure to keep the floor wet with the stripper solution during the chemical action process. If it starts to dry and stick to the floor you will have to re-apply.

Once the chemical action of the stripper has liquified the finish, you can pick up the slurry (liquified floor finish and stripper) with a wet-dry vacuum or a floor squeegee and a dustpan. Finish off the job by rinsing twice (using a neutralizing solution) and drying with a damp mop, as you would when machine stripping. Once the floor is dry it is ready for sealer or finish.

On very bad floors with a lot of build-up you may need to apply the stripper several times, or use a doodle pad to agitate the stripping solution. Occasionally you may run across a really hard case where you wind up having to use a machine to get the last of the finish up. But even in these cases the no-scrub stripper helps to break down the worst of the build-up, making it easier to get the last of it up with the machine.

MACHINELESS-RINSELESS STRIPPING

First came the machineless strippers, now we have machineless-rinseless strippers! These new strippers work the same as the machineless variety, except that as soon as the stripping solution is picked up and the floor is dry you can apply the floor finish. No rinsing or neutralizing solution is required. This is possible because the PH level of the rinseless stripper is compatible with most sealers and finishes.

Many cleaning contractors have found that the new machineless and machineless-rinseless strippers are taking a lot of the sweat, time and expense out of stripping.

HIGH SPEED FLOOR MAINTENANCE

High speed floor maintenance is a relatively new development in floor care, brought about by the invention of the high speed floor machine. These new machines have made it faster, easier and less expensive to maintain hard floors on a large scale. The new high speed technology has made it possible to "burnish" floors to a high, mirror-like shine not possible with conventional equipment.

High speed floor maintenance requires special machines and floor care products combined into a **floor care system**. The four basic components of a high speed floor care system are:

1. A high speed floor machine (burnisher).
2. Pads designed specifically for high speed burnishing and spray buffing.
3. High speed rated floor finish.
4. High speed gloss restorer.

HIGH SPEED FLOOR MACHINES (BURNISHERS) operate at speeds of 1,000 to 3,000 RPM's. When you buff a floor at these speeds you get a much higher gloss than you can achieve with a conventional buffer. This super high gloss is often referred to as the "wet look" because floors that have been burnished are so shiny they appear to be wet. You often see the wet look in supermarkets and department stores.

There is a lot of confusing terminology surrounding the new high speed equipment. "High speed", "super high speed", "ultra high speed" and "hyper speed" are all terms coined by equipment manufacturers to designate floor machines of progressively higher RPM's. Basically, the higher the RPM's, the faster the machine can produce the brilliant, "wet look" shine.

Besides higher speed there are three important differences between the conventional floor machines and the high speed machines:

1. Conventional machines are powered by electricity. High speed machines may be electric, battery powered or propane powered.

2. Conventional machines are operated in a side-to-side fashion. Burnishers are straight line machines — you push the machine straight ahead as you would a lawn mower.

3. While conventional machines are all-purpose machines, the new high speed floor burnishers are very specialized machines used solely for putting a high gloss on hard floors, either by dry burnishing or spray buffing. You cannot use the ultra high speed equipment for such maintenance tasks as stripping or bonnet cleaning.

HIGH SPEED FLOOR PADS — You cannot use a conventional floor pad with a high speed burnisher and expect to achieve the "wet look". Special pads have been designed to withstand the high speeds and temperatures generated by burnishing. These pads are light in color, generally champagne or peach colored, for dry burnishing and spray cleaning.

HIGH SPEED FLOOR FINISHES — Most conventional floor finishes will not hold up under the heat generated from high speed burnishing. They will powder off and leave you "burnishing" the bare floor. Special floor polishes have been formulated specifically for high speed floor care.

GLOSS RESTORERS (or rejuvenators, enhancers, recoaters) are used in high speed floor maintenance to restore the "wet look" shine without having to apply a new coat of finish. Gloss restorer can be spray buffed on when using machines up to about 1,500 RPM's. When using ultra high speed machines over 1,500 RPM's, the gloss restorer is mopped on, allowed to dry, then burnished.

HIGH SPEED FLOOR MAINTENANCE GUIDELINES

To create and maintain the mirror-like "wet look" shine, follow these basic guidelines:

1. Never try to establish a high speed program over old floor finishes. Start from scratch with a clean, stripped-down floor. Make sure you get all the old liquified wax and stripper residue picked up. Use a neutralizer. Allow the floor to dry before applying any sealer or finish.

2. If the floor is a porous type, start by sealing. Use a sealer that is compatible with the floor finish you intend to use. Allow the sealer to dry before applying finish.

3. To establish the base coat, put down **at least** three coats of ultra high speed rated floor finish. Apply the finish in thin even coats. Allow plenty of drying time between each coat. (Follow manufacturer's recommendations.)

4. Dry buff (burnish) the finish with a high speed floor machine once it has thoroughly dried. Check the label on the floor finish for instructions on how long to wait after application before burnishing. (Some products have to "cure" for a week or so.) Always dust mop after burnishing.

5. Apply gloss restorer and burnish as required to maintain the shine. Make sure the floor is clean before applying restorer and burnishing. This is important because the heat generated from burnishing will literally meld the loose dirt and grit into the floor finish and gradually spoil the clear, glass-like appearance you want.

6. Maintain the floor daily by dust mopping and damp mopping as necessary.

PURCHASING FLOOR CARE EQUIPMENT

There are hundreds of different conventional and high speed floor machines on the market today. Most brands are extremely durable and with proper care will give you a decade or more of reliable service. However, in buying a new one it is always a good idea to check on service availability.

New conventional floor machines start at around $500, while a new 20" 1,500 RPM burnisher starts at about $800. If you cannot find what you want locally, take a look at the machines and prices offered by the mail order suppliers listed in the Resources chapter.

When purchasing more expensive floor care equipment you can also look for distributors who will sell to you on a lease purchase basis. You can make a small down payment and pay off the balance over a period of months. If the new equipment allows you to work faster or to get new types of accounts, it will pay for itself very quickly.

If you are operating on a limited budget, a floor machine may be rented in the beginning until you can afford one or find a good used buy.

HIGH SPEED OR CONVENTIONAL — WHICH TO BUY?

When deciding which type of floor machine to buy (conventional or high speed), you should first consider your floor care needs. Do you need a specialized machine (burnisher) to achieve the "wet look" on your hard floor accounts? Or do you need an all-purpose machine (conventional) to take care of a wide variety of floor maintenance jobs? Or do you need both types of equipment? Your decision will depend on the kind of work you do and on the size of your business.

Generally, a beginning contractor should start out with a standard (175 RPM) floor machine. This is an all-purpose machine that you can use for stripping, scrubbing, polishing (buffing), spray buffing, carpet shampooing and bonnet cleaning. With an all-purpose machine you will be set to handle most small and medium-sized floor maintenance jobs that come along.

TYPES OF FLOORS

The first step in any floor maintenance operation is to identify the type of floor you are dealing with. Obviously not all floors are alike and neither are the methods required to maintain them. The three basic types of floors are:

1. Resilient Floors
   (Asphalt tile, rubber tile, linoleum and vinyl)

2. Non-Resilient or Hard Floors
   (Ceramic and quarry tile, terrazzo, marble and concrete)

3. Wood Floors.

RESILIENT FLOORS

ASPHALT TILE — This is an old-fashioned floor covering often seen in older tract homes, schools, hotels, etc. It is rarely found in newer construction. You can quickly spot asphalt tile because it comes in 9" squares, as opposed to the 12" squares of more modern floor coverings. The main thing to watch out for with asphalt tile is solvents. Paint thinner, gasoline or any solvent-based floor finish or cleaner will literally eat up this tile.

Asphalt tile should be sealed and waxed, but make sure you use a sealer and a finish that are compatible with asphalt tile — NO SOLVENTS. If uncertain, ask your janitorial supplier. Once sealed and waxed, the floor can be maintained by dust mopping, damp mopping and buffing.

In dust mopping, make sure you don't use an oily treatment that could damage the floor. In cleaning the floor, use only a neutral detergent. Special care should be taken not to allow water to sit too long on this type of flooring.

RUBBER TILE — Like asphalt tile, rubber tile reacts violently to solvents. Generally it is not necessary to seal a rubber floor. Several coats of finish (not solvent-based) will provide an easy-to-maintain surface.

The floor may be swept, damp mopped and buffed as required. Strip when necessary with an appropriate stripping solution. Avoid overwetting. Do not use oily or greasy mop treatments, or strong alkaline cleaners. Above all, remember — use no solvents.

LINOLEUM — The familiar flooring that many of us grew up on. Linoleum should be sealed and waxed. Be very careful not to overwet linoleum as it is highly susceptible to water damage. In scrubbing, use as little water as possible. On a large linoleum surface, clean it in sections so that you can pick up the water quickly. Use a neutral detergent and don't use any products containing alkali. Avoid ammonia and scouring powder as well.

For regular maintenance, linoleum may be dust mopped and damp mopped when necessary

VINYL TILE — Vinyl is the bright, colorful tile found everywhere. Vinyl tile comes in thousands of embossed designs and patterns, often imitating brick, wood or stone. If you do residential work, this is the tile you will run into most often on kitchen and bathroom floors.

Vinyl tile will not usually require sealing and in fact, much of this modern tile comes "factory sealed", or so they say. Several coats of floor finish will improve the appearance and maintenance ease of most vinyl floors, particularly if they get a lot of traffic.

Floors should be swept regularly to remove the gritty soil that works like sandpaper. It may be easier to use a vacuum to get all the dirt out of the indented areas in the patterns. In scrubbing operations it is helpful to have a wet-dry vacuum to pull the water out of the patterned areas.

Sweeping and damp mopping with plain water and a neutral detergent are adequate for day-to-day care. As with all resilient floors, take care not to flood the vinyl when scrubbing and stripping.

Fortunately for the beginner, vinyl tile is more "forgiving" than most floor materials. It is hard to find a way to ruin it, as long as you don't get it too wet.

NON-RESILIENT (HARD) FLOORS

CERAMIC TILE — Ceramic tile is a very common floor covering. This is the kind of tile you often find on restroom floors in little 1" to 2" squares. Another form of ceramic tile is quarry tile. Quarry tile comes in larger square, rectangular or hexagonal shapes, usually reddish or brown in color. Unglazed quarry tile is often installed in restaurant kitchens, lobbies and other heavy traffic areas.

Ceramic tile is a very hard floor surface which resists virtually all stains, and therefore normally requires no sealing or waxing. Depending on the amount of soil, a ceramic floor may be swept with a broom, damp mopped, wet mopped or scrubbed. In scrubbing, do not use steel wool pads or scouring powder.

In cleaning ceramic or quarry tile in greasy commercial kitchens, a detergent containing degreaser in hot water can be used. First, spread the degreaser solution with a wet mop over the entire kitchen floor. Let it sit a minute and then pick it up with a wrung-out mop. A slight film may be left, but this is usually not a problem in a workroom area. If it is, rinse the floor once with clear, hot water and damp mop dry.

The only difficulty in maintaining quarry tile is keeping the grouting between the tiles looking good. This cement grouting is porous and stains rather easily. After a while, the stained grouting starts to make the whole floor look unclean. To prevent staining in the first place, the floor can be sealed with a terrazzo or concrete sealer. One coat should do it.

TERRAZZO — Terrazzo is a beautiful flooring composed of marble chips set in cement. This type of flooring has become very popular and is commonly seen in shopping malls, restaurants, banks, department stores, etc. Terrazzo is a "favorite", next to carpet, with many professional cleaners because of its brilliant appearance and relative ease of maintenance.

The best thing that can be done for a terrazzo floor is to use a penetrating terrazzo sealer, followed by several coats of compatible floor finish. This protects the floor, enhances its appearance and makes your maintenance job much easier.

Terrazzo may be dust mopped (non-oily treatment), damp mopped, buffed, scrubbed and stripped as required. Spray buffing is highly effective. The most important thing to remember in working with terrazzo is to avoid using cleaners containing alkali or acids. All cleaning solutions should be neutral. Alkali products in particular have defaced many an expensive slab of terrazzo.

You see this in restrooms where someone has attempted to "scrub this floor clean once and for all" using scouring powder, which is highly alkaline. The result is a badly scarred and pock-marked floor. No amount of sealing or waxing can restore this floor to life. Care also needs to be taken not to splash toilet bowl cleaner (acid) on terrazzo floors in restrooms. Maintaining terrazzo is not hard. The three main points to remember are:

1. Use a neutral cleaning product. If this is not clearly stated on the label, ask your supplier.
2. Seal the floor with a penetrating type of terrazzo sealer.
3. Keep all alkali, acids and oils off the floor. Do not use steel wool pads.

CONCRETE — Concrete floors are commonly found in industrial operations, workrooms, shops, garages, warehouses — any place that requires a flooring that can take some punishment. Concrete should be sealed with a concrete sealer to keep down "dusting" of the cement. Sealing also fills the pores and creates a smooth, easy-to-maintain surface.

Concrete floors should be etched with a muriatic acid solution prior to sealing. This removes the surface layer of cement which can keep the sealer from bonding properly to the concrete. Muriatic acid contains hydrochloric acid, and **extreme care must be taken in the handling and use of it.** Consult your supplier and the product label for specific instructions on the product you are using. Muriatic acid can also be used to remove cement and concrete from brick or tile floors, a common problem in new construction clean-up.

The floor must be dry and clean before any sealer can be applied. Scrub with a regular stripping solution or a specially formulated concrete cleaner. Once sealed, the floor may be waxed and buffed if required for appearance or heavy wear. Do not attempt to wax an unsealed concrete floor. For regular maintenance a concrete floor may be swept with a push broom (or a dust mop if the floor is smooth). Heavier soil can be removed by mopping or machine scrubbing.

MARBLE — The "museum floor" also found in banks and classy hotels, offices, restaurants and stores. Despite its rock-hard appearance, marble is not stain proof. For this reason, marble floors should be sealed with a penetrating type of sealer or "marble impregnator". This will protect the floor and make it easier to maintain.

In cleaning a marble floor, **never use any solution containing an acid.** Also avoid highly abrasive cleaning methods or materials that could scratch the smooth marble surface. Do not use steel wool as this may cause rust stains. For daily care the floor may be dust mopped (non-oily treatment) and damp mopped. Plain water is often adequate. A mild synthetic detergent may be used for scrubbing. A sealed marble floor may be buffed to bring out the beauty of the marble.

NOTE: Marble is an **expensive** type of flooring. This is not a floor to "practise" on! Seek professional assistance from a hard floor expert. Consult your supplier for recommendations.

WOOD FLOORS

Wood floors should be sealed for their protection as well as for proper maintenance. Special wood sealers are made for this purpose. Wood is also sometimes treated with other products, including lacquer, shellac, varnish and urethane.

When sealing a new wood floor, first make sure it is clean, dry and clear of all dust. Thorough vacuuming is best. Be sure you've got adequate ventilation, because wood sealer contains solvents. Spread the sealer on with a large lamb's wool applicator. A second coat may be applied after the first has dried. Check the instructions on the product you are using for recommended drying times. Once sealed, the floor may be polished with one or more coats of a **solvent-based** wax, either paste or liquid. Never apply this wax to an unsealed floor.

For regular maintenance, wood floors may be dust mopped (light wax treatment) or vacuumed, and dry buffed. Always dust mop after buffing. A damp mop, wrung out to the maximum, can be used for spot cleaning, but be careful — water and wood floors don't mix. When complete cleaning is required, you should use a specially formulated solvent-based wood cleaner.

Chapter 13
BOOKKEEPING

Recordkeeping for a service business (sole proprietorship or partnership) can be very simple. There are no hard and fast rules about how to keep your books. The main requirement is that you keep an **accurate** record of all your income, expenses and deductions.

You must keep good daily records, even if you employ a bookkeeper periodically. Keeping good books is obviously helpful at tax time, but most important, it allows you to monitor your business on a daily basis. By keeping good records you will gain a real understanding of where the money is coming from and where it is going.

SETTING UP YOUR BOOKKEEPING SYSTEM

There are two ways to go about setting up your books. You can buy a complete bookkeeping system at an office supply store or you can buy ordinary accounting paper and make up your own system.

The trouble with the store-bought systems is that they aren't designed for your particular business needs. For this reason many small business owners prefer to buy columnar paper and customize their bookkeeping system to suit their own business. The bookkeeping examples in this chapter have been prepared on ordinary columnar paper which can be purchased at any stationery store.

Most small service businesses use a **single entry** bookkeeping system. This means you only make one entry in your books for each item of income or expense. Service businesses also usually keep their books on a **cash basis.** This means you record your income when you actually receive the payment and record your expenses as they are taken (when the check is actually written).

The basic records required by a sole proprietorship or partnership are Cash Receipts Journal, Expense Journal and Annual Summary. You will also need your business checking account.

BUSINESS CHECKING ACCOUNT

Your bookkeeping system begins with and is built around your business checking account. If you try to operate out of your personal checking account you are asking for Trouble, with a capital "T"! All of your business income should be channeled through your business account.

Pay as many of your expenses as possible by check. The checks, along with your sales slips, receipts, etc., serve to document your business expenses to the IRS, should you ever be audited.

Don't pay any personal bills out of your business checking account if you can avoid it — it clutters up your finances. When you want to withdraw money from your business account for personal use, write a check to yourself and record it as "Owner's Drawing" or "Withdrawal".

PETTY CASH

Petty cash is a convenient way of keeping track of little deductible expenses that are too small to write a check for. To establish a petty cash fund you simply write a business check. Make the check out to "Petty Cash" and cash it at your bank. The fund can be any size — $25 is common. Get the money in small change and one dollar bills. Put the $25 in a small box or drawer and use it to pay for small miscellaneous items that you need for the business (vacuum cleaner belts, postage, key duplicating, etc.)

In this box also place a pad of petty cash vouchers, available at a stationery store, or just a plain note pad. Whenever you make a small cash purchase be sure to get a receipt. Make a note on the voucher pad of the date, amount and item purchased and reimburse yourself from the fund. Attach your receipt to the voucher and store it with the money.

When the fund starts to run low, add up the expenses and make out another check to Petty Cash for the exact amount you spent. Cash the check and put the money back in the fund. The amount of cash in the fund and the total of expenses on the vouchers should always equal $25 (or whatever amount you establish).

CASH RECEIPTS JOURNAL

The Cash Receipts Journal is a record of all your business income. (See example, page 193) Whether you get paid by cash or check, you are required to keep track of it all. It may be helpful to divide your income up by contract and one-time jobs.

It is a good idea to record your income in the Cash Receipts Journal the same day you receive it, or at least before you deposit the check. Otherwise it is easy to lose track of when your invoices were paid, how much was paid, etc.

The Cash Receipts Journal is the most important (and interesting!) part of your bookkeeping system. It tells you how much money you are grossing month by month, which months are slow and which are strong, what percentage of your income is contract work and what percentage is one-time jobs.

Making entries in your Cash Receipts Journal is one bookkeeping chore you should find enjoyable!

EXPENSE JOURNAL

The Expense Journal is a complete day-by-day record of all your business expenses. (See example, page 194)

To set up your Expense Journal, first take a look at your business and decide how many types of expenses you will have on a regular basis. Then buy the columnar paper that has enough columns to accommodate your needs. Designate one column for each of your regular expenses. Infrequent expense items that do not warrant a column of their own are entered in the "Miscellaneous" column. The example on page 194 is set up for the types of expenses typical in a small janitorial business. However your needs may differ somewhat and you should customize your Expense Journal to suit your own business. For instance, if you work regularly with subcontractors you will need a column for "Contract Labor" or "Subcontracts". And if you deduct actual auto expenses, as opposed to the standard mileage rate, you will need a column for "Automobile".

Most of the entries in your Expense Journal will come directly from your business checkbook. When you write a check be sure to include a brief description of what it was for, along with the check number, amount of the check, date written and to whom paid. Then periodically take a few minutes and transfer this information to your Expense Journal, entering each expense in the appropriate column. How often you need to copy ("post") the checkbook entries into your Expense Journal will depend on how many checks you are writing. But be sure to post your Expense Journal at least once a month. Otherwise you start to fall too far behind and the chance of error increases.

Petty cash vouchers should also be totalled periodically and the total entered in the Expense Journal. Distribute the petty cash expenses in their appropriate columns and lump the odd ones under Miscellaneous.

Occasionally you may need to use cash, a money order or a personal check for a business expense. When you do this be sure to enter the expense as soon as possible in your Expense Journal, before you lose track of it.

If you are uncertain as to whether or not an expense is deductible, go ahead and get a receipt and record it in the Expense Journal, under the Miscellaneous column. When tax time comes your tax preparer will be able to determine if you can deduct it or not.

At the end of the month, total each column in the Expense Journal. Double check your addition by comparing the total of the "Check Amount" column with the total of all the other columns combined. These should be the same. If not, go back and locate the error.

The monthly totals in your Expense Journal give you an exact accounting of where your money is going. When you compare the monthly totals in your Expense Journal with the monthly totals in your Cash Receipts Journal you have a good picture of your cash flow situation.

ANNUAL SUMMARY (MONTHLY TOTALS RECORD)

Expenses and income should be totaled each month and entered in an Annual Summary or Monthly Totals Record. (See example, page 195) These monthly totals give you an idea of your profit.

At the end of the year, total all the columns (and double check) and you've got most of the information you need for your income tax preparation, already totalled and itemized.

FINANCIAL STATEMENTS

The two common types of financial statements are the balance sheet (statement of assets and liabilities) and the profit and loss statement (income statement). They are useful in analyzing your business's condition and progress.

A balance sheet lists your assets (what you own), your liabilities (what you owe) and your net worth (the difference between your assets and your liabilities).

The profit and loss statement shows your net income for a specific period of time. Your gross income less all your expenses equals your net profit. The monthly totals in your Cash Receipts Journal less the totals in your Expense Journal give you a rough profit and loss statement. (To get an exact statement you need to add in **all your business expenses** such as depreciation for the period, automobile expenses, etc.)

If you are a sole proprietorship, you probably won't need a balance sheet, and you will already have a good idea of your profit from your Monthly Totals Record. However, if you intend to borrow money from the bank you will definitely need financial statements. Hire an accountant or bookkeeper to prepare them for you. If you have kept your books in good shape he or she will have no trouble preparing the statements.

WHERE TO GO FOR HELP

If you are unsure of how to get your bookkeeping system set up, or how to use the one you've got, don't hesitate to seek professional help. This is much too critical an aspect of your business to be left to guesswork — poor record-keeping is one of the main causes of small business failure.

There are many books available in the library that contain good general information on bookkeeping for the small business. One excellent book is *Small Time Operator, How To Start Your Own Small Business, Keep Your Books, Pay Your Taxes, and Stay Out of Trouble!* (See "Start-Up Information" in the Resources chapter.)

1989 DATE	January 1989 CASH RECEIPTS JOURNAL DESCRIPTION	JOB	CONTRACT
1	Jan 2	Window Cleaning - Jefferson	4500	
2	2	Johnson Building		10000
3	2	Construction Clean-up - Davis	18500	
4	3	Nelson + Nelson (final payment)		42500
5	5	Reed Pharmacy		7500
6	10	Clubhouse		12500
7	10	2 Star Restaurant (incl. windows)		40000
8	10	Window Cleaning - Fletcher	3000	
9	11	Apartment cleaned (vacant) - Marvin	6500	
10	11	Window Cleaning - Springer	4500	
11	12	Window Cleaning - Martin	2500	
12	14	Western Shop		9500
13	16	742 10th Avenue - strip + wax	7500	
14	16	Tower Building		100000
15	18	Construction Clean-up - Phillips	8000	
16	18	Regent Building		80000
17	20	Palomar Shop (adjusted)		7500
18	20	Engineering Company		20000
19	21	Window Cleaning - Saul	6500	
20	23	First Bank		40000
21	27	Marshell's		24500
22	29	Pizza Parlor (November)		32500
23	31	Colony Room (2 months)		60000
24		January Subtotals	61500	48 6500
25		JANUARY TOTAL		548000
26				
27				
28				
29				

CASH RECEIPTS JOURNAL

Prepared By
Approved By
Initials   Date

DATE 1989	Paid To	Ck #	1 Amount	2 Janitorial Supplies	3 Janitorial Equipment	4 Advertising	5 Office Supplies	6 Net Payroll	7 Taxes	8 Phone	9 Owner's Drawing	10 Insurance	11 Postage	12 Miscellaneous Description	13 Amount
Jan 1	Janitorial Supply	122	52.00	52.00											
2	Jonathan Doe	123	425.00					425.00							
3	Insurance (Bond)	124	85.00									85.00			
5	IRS	125	175.00						175.00						
5	Dept of Benefit Payments	126	105.00						105.00						
7	Petty Cash	127	20.00				5.00						5.00	Key Duplication	5.00
9	Owner's Drawing	128	500.00								500.00				
10	Janitorial Supply (vacuum)	129	250.00		250.00										
11	Daily Times	130	50.00			50.00									
14	Telephone Company	131	42.00							42.00					
16	Jonathan Doe	132	430.00					430.00							
18	Stationers	133	40.00				40.00								
19	Vacuum Repair Shop	134	35.00											Vacuum Repair	35.00
20	Rental Yard	135	40.00											Equipment Rental	40.00
22	Janitorial Supply (wet-dry vac)	136	300.00		300.00										
23	Petty Cash	137	15.00											P.O. Box Rental	10.00
24	Daily Times	138	50.00			50.00									
26	Owner's Drawing	139	1000.00								1000.00				
28	Insurance	140	5.00									5.00			
30	Bank Service Charge	—	5.00											Service Charge	5.00
	TOTALS		3669.00	62.00	550.00	100.00	45.00	855.00	280.00	42.00	1500.00	135.00	5.00		95.00

8473 BUFF · 8473 GREEN · 8273 WHITE

ANNUAL SUMMARY

1989	Income	Checks *	Janitorial Supplies	Janitorial Equipment	Advertising	Office Supplies	Net Payroll	Taxes	Phone	Owner's Drawing	Insurance *	Postage	Misc.
January	54800	3663.00	62.00	55.00	100.00	45.00	855.00	28.00	42.00	150.00	135.00	5.00	9.5
February	3759.00												
March	3310.00												
April	4725.00												
May	3625.00												
June	5050.00												
July	4840.00												
August	6250.00												
September	5250.00												
October	6040.00												
November	5090.00												
December	6000.00												
TOTALS	59519.00	51083.00	744.00	2545.00	1200.0	540.00	12000.00	1550.00	504.00	2800.00	1200.00	100.00	2680.00

(* Checks — includes owner's drawing)

(* Insurance — includes Workmen's Comp.)

ANNUAL SUMMARY

Chapter 14
TAXES

> **NOTE:** This chapter is intended to provide general information on tax situations commonly encountered by the small cleaning contractor. It is not intended to cover every situation nor could it possibly do so. The reader should keep in mind that tax laws change all the time and the information in this chapter concerning specific tax regulations is current only up to the date of printing. It should also be understood that the publisher and author are not engaged in rendering legal, accounting or tax consulting services. If accounting or tax advice is required, the services of a competent tax advisor should be sought. (See "Finding a Good Tax Preparer" later in this chapter.)

When you are in business for yourself you are entitled to a number of income tax write-offs (deductions) not available to the employee. Automobile expenses and home office deductions are just two of the tax breaks available to you as a self-employed business person. Every legitimate business expense you take reduces your taxable income and saves you money at tax time.

You must keep accurate records of all your business-related expenses. To satisfy the IRS you should document each of your expenses with some form of material proof — a cash receipt, cancelled check, mileage record, petty cash voucher, sales slip, etc. Save these receipts with your tax records. Your receipts should, of course, match up with your journal entries.

WHAT CAN YOU DEDUCT?

According to the IRS, "To be deductible, a business expense must be both ordinary and necessary. An **ordinary** expense is one that is common and accepted in your field of business, trade or profession. A **necessary** expense is one that is helpful and appropriate for your trade, business or profession. An expense does not have to be indispensable to be considered necessary...If you have an expense that is partly for business and partly personal, you must separate the personal part from the business part."

Some of the expenses commonly taken in professional cleaning are:

payroll	employer taxes
equipment (depreciation)	office supplies
janitorial supplies	advertising
equipment rental	post office box
telephone	key duplication
postage	business taxes
uniforms	printing
interest expense	repairs
consultants	automobile expense
bonding	professional fees
tax preparation	bank service charges
bookkeeping service	business licenses
collection expenses	sales commissions
conventions	business credit card fees
car wash	education expense
electricity	fire insurance
trash service	fees for services
legal expenses	liability insurance
answering service	payments to subcontractors
secretarial service	dues to business associations
laundry and cleaning	meals and entertainment (80%)
trade magazines	Workmen's Compensation
travel	office furniture (depreciation)
home office	permits
publications	reference books
rent	sales tax
stationery	utilities
copying	casualty losses
this book	

This list is by no means exhaustive. A very thorough explanation of business expenses can be found in IRS Publication #535, "Business Expenses".

SOME EXPENSES YOU CAN'T WRITE OFF

Not every business-related expense is deductible. Here are the most common exceptions:

Meals — You can't write off your lunch. However, if you take a client to lunch and discuss business you can write off 80% of the cost, as long as the expense is not "extravagant". The 80% rule also applies to your food expenses when you are on a business trip away from your home.

Clothing is not deductible, unless you have regular work uniforms.

Commuting expenses — The cost of driving back and forth to an office is not deductible. (If you have an office in your home you have no commuting expenses — all your business-related mileage is deductible.)

Owner's drawing — You cannot take a deduction for money you draw out of your business. Nor can you take a deduction for a salary you pay yourself, unless you are incorporated.

Taxes — Federal income tax and self-employment taxes are not deductible. But you can deduct your state income tax on your personal federal income tax return.

Parking violations, fines and speeding tickets are not deductible, even if they occur while you are on business.

Charitable contributions or gifts are not deductible to your business (unless you are incorporated), but may be deductible on your personal return. However if your contribution serves to promote your business it can be written off as advertising — for example, sponsoring a Little League team.

Loans — The principal portion of a business loan is not deductible, only the interest.

Life insurance premiums — Premiums on a life insurance policy covering yourself, an employee, or any person financially interested in your business are not deductible if you are directly or indirectly a beneficiary of the policy.

Land — Buildings are depreciated, but the land they sit on is not. For example, if you have a home office and want to depreciate it, you can only write off a portion of the value of your house, apart from the land it sits on.

Fixed assets — With some exceptions equipment that you buy for your business must be depreciated over a number of years rather than written off as an expense. See the discussion of depreciation that follows.

DEPRECIATION

Pieces of equipment you buy for your business that have a useful life of one year or more may need to be depreciated rather than expensed. This means that instead of writing their cost off right away you must spread the expense out over a number of years, deducting a portion each year. Currently most new janitorial equipment, autos, trucks, typewriters, computers, etc. must be depreciated over a five or seven year period.

You can also take a deduction for personal items that you convert to business use. For instance, if you set up a home office and use a desk that you previously had elsewhere in the house, you can establish a fair market value for the desk and include it on your depreciation schedule.

You can also take a deduction for items that you use partly for business and partly for personal use. But your depreciation deduction is limited to the percentage of business use. For example, if you use a home computer 75% of the time for business and your kids use it 25% of the time for computer games you can depreciate 75% of its value. However there are limitations on items you use less than 50% of the time for business.

Keep a record of all equipment purchases from the time you start your business. The basic information you need in your equipment record is:

1. Description of the equipment.
2. The date the equipment was purchased or acquired.
3. The total cost of the equipment (including sales tax).

Your equipment record provides you with the information you need to claim the correct amount of depreciation on your tax return. Keep up-to-date equipment records and your tax preparer will have no trouble determining the correct depreciation deductions.

The main drawback with depreciating equipment is that you have to spend the money now but you can't take the tax deduction now. Fortunately there is a way, (as of this writing at least), to deduct the cost of up to $10,000 of equipment in the same year you purchase it. It's called the Section 179 Deduction.

THE SECTION 179 DEDUCTION

Under a special section of the depreciation rules, the Section 179 Deduction, you have the option to write off up to $10,000 of depreciable assets in the same year you put them to use in your business. (The write-off is limited to $5,000 if you are married and filing separately.) To take this deduction you must elect to treat the purchase as an expense rather than as a depreciable asset. Any equipment you purchase over the $10,000 limit must be depreciated as usual.

There are a number of limitations on the Section 179 Deduction. For example, the amount that you write off cannot be more than your taxable business income for the year (figured without the 179 Deduction). In other words, the assets you choose to expense cannot cause you to have a business loss. If the deduction you want to take exceeds your taxable income you can carry the balance (up to the $10,000 limit) over to the next tax year. There are also limits on the amount of Section 179 Deduction you can take on a passenger car used in your business.

To get all the details on depreciation and the Section 179 Deduction see IRS publication #334, "Tax Guide for Small Business", or Publication #534, "Depreciation". Both are available free of charge from the IRS.

NOTE: If you are just starting out and haven't made much money in your first year, it may be to your advantage to depreciate your equipment rather than take the 179 Deduction. You will then have deductions in later years, when you will need them to offset your growing income. Talk it over with your tax preparer.

BUSINESS USE OF YOUR HOME

If you have an area of your home that you can set aside as your business office, you can take a number of deductions at tax time. Your home office must meet certain tests to qualify:

1. You must use the office **exclusively and regularly** in connection with your business. "Exclusively" means that you must use a specific part of your home only for the purpose of carrying on your business. If you use part of your home as your business office and also use it for personal purposes you have not met the exclusive use test. For instance you cannot deduct for a den that you use as an office and a part-time sewing room. "Regular" use simply means that you use the office on a regular basis, not just occasionally.

2. To deduct for a home office it must be used as **your principal place of business.** Usually if you have an office downtown and one at home you will not be able to deduct for the home office. However there are exceptions. If you do most of your work out of your home office, or meet clients there, you may still be able to deduct it even though you also have an office outside the home.

You can also take a deduction for a separate, free-standing structure such as a guest house, studio or garage, if you use the structure exclusively and regularly for your business. This structure does not have to be your principal place of business.

WHICH COSTS CAN YOU DEDUCT?

To determine how much you can deduct for your home office you must first calculate the percentage of space in your home you are using for business. To do this you divide the area set aside for your office by the total square footage of your home. For instance, if you use 150 square feet for your office and your home is 1,500 square feet, you are using 10% of your home for business (150 divided by 1,500).

You can also figure business use by the number of rooms in your home, if the rooms in your home are approximately the same size. For example, if you have a five room home and you use one room for business, you are using 20% of your home for business.

Once you determine what percentage of your home is deductible for business you simply multiply that percentage times your deductible home maintenance expenses. For instance, if you paid $10,000 in home mortgage interest and you used 20% of your home for business, you could deduct $2,000 for your home office (20% x $10,000). Examples of household expenses you can deduct are:

1. Mortgage interest or rent
2. Real estate taxes
3. Insurance
4. Utilities and services
5. Depreciation
6. Repairs
7. Casualty losses (theft, fire, etc.)
8. Security systems

To be deductible these expenses must be related in some way to the part of your home used for business.

In addition to taking a percentage of your overall home maintenance expenses you can also deduct (or depreciate) the full amount of any expenses you spend specifically on the office portion of your home, such as paint, carpeting, mini-blinds, etc. All of your office furnishings are also deductible, of course, as business assets.

Not all home-related expenses are deductible and there are limitations that apply if you show a business loss. Also you should be aware that depreciating a portion of your house for a home office has certain tax consequences when you decide to sell the house. To get all the details on having a home office, read IRS Publication # 587, "Business Use of Your Home".

AUTOMOBILE EXPENSES

If you are a small contractor working on your own, automobile expenses will represent one of your biggest tax write-offs. Even if you use your car part of the time for business and part for personal, you are still entitled to deduct that portion of the expenses that went for business use. There are two ways of deducting auto expenses — you can either keep track of your **actual automobile expenses** or you can use the **standard mileage rate.**

If you choose to calculate your automobile deduction using your actual expenses, the items you must keep track of are gas, oil, repairs, insurance, tires, interest on your car loan, depreciation, taxes, licenses, garage, rent, parking fees, tolls and maintenance. You can buy an automobile expense record book at any stationery store — keep this log in your glove compartment to record your daily automobile expenses, and be sure to save all your receipts.

Keeping track of all these miscellaneous automobile expenses can be quite a chore. To simplify things, or to get a larger deduction, many business people use the standard mileage rate to figure their car expenses.

THE STANDARD MILEAGE RATE

The IRS currently allows you to deduct 24¢ a mile for the first 15,000 business miles you drive each year, and 11¢ a mile for each additional business mile. For example, if you put on 19,000 business miles in a year, you could deduct $4,040 at tax time (24¢ x 15,000 = $3,600 plus 11¢ x 4,000 = $440).

When you use the standard mileage rate you may still deduct your auto loan interest, parking fees and tolls, and any state or local taxes on your car. This is **in addition** to the standard mileage rate.

There are a number of conditions and limits placed on using the standard mileage rate:

1. You must own the car.

2. You must not use the car for hire.

3. You must not operate a fleet of cars using two or more at the same time.

4. You may not claim depreciation or the Section 179 deduction (depreciation is considered to be included in the standard mileage rate).

5. You must choose to use the standard mileage rate in the first year that you use the car in your business. If you do not choose the standard mileage rate in the first year you cannot use it for that car in any later year.

When you use the standard mileage rate your car is considered fully depreciated after you have driven 60,000 **business** miles. However, no more than 15,000 business miles per year will be counted against the 60,000 miles, no matter how many business miles you actually drive in the year. Once your car is considered fully depreciated you may only take 11¢ per mile for any business miles you drive.

If you use more than one car on an **alternating basis**, the total mileage of both cars must be combined to figure the 15,000 mile annual limit at the 24¢ mileage rate. However, if one car is already considered fully depreciated do not combine the total business miles of both cars, because you may only take 11¢ a mile for the depreciated car.

To claim the standard mileage rate deduction you need to keep accurate records of your business mileage. You can do this by keeping an automobile mileage record in your car.

AUTOMOBILE MILEAGE RECORD

Here is a simple way to keep track of your business miles. Place a small, lined notepad in the glove compartment of your vehicle. At the start of each business trip record the date, starting mileage and destination. At the end of the trip write in the ending mileage and the total mileage. When you use the car for personal errands don't write in anything, unless you happen to be doing some business along the way.

All this takes just a few seconds a day and it gets you a 24¢ a mile deduction — well worth the effort! At the end of the year get out your adding machine and add up the total miles column. Multiply the total by 24¢ (11¢ per mile over 15,000 miles) and you've got your automobile tax deduction.

You are not required to send in your mileage records (or any other receipts) with your tax return. However, you should keep them as tangible proof if you are ever questioned or audited by the IRS.

For a full discussion of auto expenses and the standard mileage rate see the "Tax Guide for Small Business", IRS Publication # 334, under the heading "Transportation Expenses".

Date	Begin	End	Total	Mileage Record
4/10	13923	13962	39	Cleaning Route
4/12	13982	14004	22	Bank Bid -- 1040 4th St.
4/13	14016	14044	28	Window Cleaning Jobs - Davis + Martin
4/14	14044	14052	8	Stationers, Janitorial Supply
4/14	14052	14096	44	Post Office, Printer, Cleaning Route
4/15	14101	14113	12	Window Bids - Hart + Ellis
4/15	14113	14131	18	Estimate -- Paradise Hills Shopping Mall
4/16	14131	14173	42	Cleaning Route, Printer
4/17	14185	14197	12	Seal Floor - Electro Industries, Inc.
4/20	14251	14303	52	Bid - Main St. Office Complex -- Cleaning Route
4/21	14305	14325	20	Construction clean-up - airport
4/21	14325	14364	39	Cleaning Route
4/22	14370	14392	22	Restaurant Bid - Hwy. 5 + 6th Ave.

RETIREMENT PLANS FOR THE SELF-EMPLOYED

Retirement plans for the self-employed are called "Keogh" plans. Only sole proprietors and partnerships can set up a Keogh plan. There are two types of Keogh plans, the **defined contribution** plan and the **defined benefit** plan. Most small business people who have a Keogh plan choose the defined contribution plan. It is much easier to set up than the defined benefit plan and it gives you greater flexibility. Under the defined contribution plan you can contribute as much as you want toward your retirement each year (up to the allowable limit), or nothing at all if you choose.

Keogh plans are similar to the IRA plans for individuals, in that you pay no income tax on the money you invest in the plan until you withdraw it in your retirement. And, like the IRA plans, you can invest in a Keogh plan up to the date your tax return is due and have it deducted from your previous year's taxes, if you choose.

As a self-employed business person you can put a good deal more money in a Keogh plan each year than an individual can put into an IRA plan.

Currently you are allowed to invest up to $30,000 a year in a defined contribution Keogh plan, but not more than 20% of your net earnings from self-employment. Another advantage to the Keogh plan is that you can also have an IRA at the same time (subject to certain income limitations).

Putting your money in a Keogh plan is one way to reduce your taxable income, but not as much as you might at first think. Unfortunately your Keogh contributions do not reduce your self-employment taxes. You must still pay self-employment tax on your net business earnings before subtracting out the money you pay into your retirement fund.

Any money you contribute to a Keogh plan is tied up until you reach age $59\frac{1}{2}$. If you pull the money out early it is added to your taxable income for that year along with a 10% federal penalty and possible state penalties. Another point to consider is that if you have employees who have been with you a while you may have to include them in the plan and pay for their retirement benefits with your own money.

Keogh plans are available through many banks, savings and loans, insurance companies and investment firms. Not all plans are the same — if you are considering a particular retirement plan be sure it is "IRS approved". For more information on Keogh plans get IRS Publication # 560, "Self-Employed Retirement Plans".

HEALTH INSURANCE FOR THE SELF-EMPLOYED

Many insurance companies offer health insurance for self-employed individuals. The premiums are high but not unaffordable, especially if you go with a high deductible and pay your small medical expenses out-of-pocket. When shopping for a health insurance plan be sure to look for a company that is financially strong. An "A" rating is good, but an "A+" rating is better.

If you are a sole proprietor or partner you can deduct 25% of the cost of health insurance for yourself and your family. This deduction is taken as an adjustment to income on your personal income tax return. It does not reduce your business income for self-employment tax purposes. The 25% deduction is subject to the following limitations:

1. The deduction cannot be more than your net income from the business.

2. If you or your spouse works for someone else and you are eligible to participate in a health plan provided by your employer or your spouse's employer, you may not take the deduction.

3. If you have employees you cannot take the deduction unless you provide each employee with health insurance. (The cost of any health insurance you provide your employees is fully deductible to your business.)

The above limitations apply only to sole proprietors and partners. If you are incorporated you can write off 100% of your health insurance, provided you make the insurance available to your employees.

ESTIMATED TAXES

When you are self-employed you do not have an employer to withhold tax from your earnings. Instead you must make an estimate of the tax you will owe for the year and send it in to the IRS in four quarterly installments. The first installment is due on April 15th and the other three are due June 15th, September 15th and January 15th of the following year. You can use an IRS estimated tax work sheet to help estimate how much you will owe and how much your quarterly installments should be.

You submit your estimated payments each quarter using a payment voucher, Form 1040-ES. These forms are available from any IRS office or your tax preparer. Once you've made your first estimated payment you will be "in the system" and each year thereafter the IRS will send you a Form 1040-ES package, which includes an estimated tax work sheet and preprinted vouchers.

When you pay estimated taxes you must file your income tax return on the regular Form 1040 at the end of the year, rather than form 1040-A or 1040-EZ. If you owed less than $500 in tax last year, including self-employment tax, you do not have to file estimated tax payments this year.

If you pay too little estimated tax the IRS can hit you with a penalty, usually about 10% of the amount you've underpaid. However, as long as you have paid 90% of this year's tax liability (in four equal installments), there is no penalty. You can also cover yourself by paying 100% of the tax that you owed last year (in four equal installments). For example, if your total tax bill for last year was $4,000 you could simply pay $1,000 each quarter this year and there would be no penalty assessed, even though you may actually owe $5,000 this year. But you must pay the balance owing (in this case $1,000) on April 15th, along with your tax return.

You must also keep in mind that April 15th is the due date for your first quarterly payment of the present year. To cover yourself you'll need to pay one fourth of the amount of taxes you owed last year. Using the same example you would need to send in $1,250 as your first estimated payment, along with the $1,000 that you owed from last year for a total outlay of $2,250. If you are not anticipating this double payment it can come as rude shock and a real blow to your cash flow.

If your business is growing fast and you are making more money than you did last year, it would be wise to increase your estimated payments or start setting money aside for April 15th.

Estimated taxes are covered in depth in IRS Publication #505, "Tax Withholding and Estimated Taxes", free from the IRS.

SELF-EMPLOYMENT TAXES

Self-employment does not exempt you from contributing to the Social Security System. If you are a sole proprietorship or a partnership you must pay Self-Employment tax and file Schedule SE (Computation of Social Security Self-Employment Tax) along with your annual income tax return. The self-employment tax is currently 13.02% of the first $48,000 you make, zero thereafter.

If you are required to file estimated tax (Form 1040-ES) you must include an estimate of your self-employment tax on that form and pay it quarterly along with your estimated income tax.

Self-employment tax is not one of the highlights of self-employment. When you're in business for yourself you put in long hours, take the risks involved in having your own business and provide jobs for others. Yet, as a self-employed business person you pay a higher rate of social security tax than any other member of society, 13.02% as opposed to 7.51% for the employee. And the self-employment tax is **in addition** to your income tax, making it a form of double taxation on your business earnings.

So — sharpen your pencil and look for every legitimate tax deduction available to you. If you don't, you're paying more tax than you should.

FINDING A GOOD TAX PREPARER

Many small business people do their own taxes. But filling out tax forms is time-consuming and tedious work. Even after spending days pouring over IRS forms and booklets you're liable to miss a tax deduction you could have taken. It's not your fault — no one but a full-time accountant or tax preparer has the time to keep up with the ever-changing volume of tax laws. That's why a tax specialist can save you time and money.

How do you go about finding a good tax preparer? First of all, don't go to one of the mass production tax preparation services you see advertised on TV.

All they can usually do is take the numbers you give them and plug them into the standard IRS forms. True, they will do your taxes cheaply, but you'll get what you pay for. What you need is a tax preparer who will take the time to look closely at your business and dig out every tax savings available to you.

The best way to find the right tax preparer is to talk with other small business people, especially people in service businesses, and see who they use. You don't necessarily need a C.P.A., but you do want someone who has experience doing taxes for small businesses.

Be sure to interview a tax preparer, either in person or over the phone, before using their services. Look for someone you can talk to and understand. The best professionals in any field have the ability to make the complexities of their specialized field understandable to the layman. Avoid those "professionals" who talk jargon and throw a lot of big words at you. The tax preparer you decide to work with should be someone you can call on for advice on any tax or accounting problems that come up during the year, not just at tax time.

STAYING ON TOP OF THE TAX SITUATION

Well before the end of the year you should take stock of your tax situation and make a rough estimate of how much tax you are going to owe on April 15. If it looks like you are going to owe the IRS a substantial amount of money, there are several things you can do to help yourself. One of the advantages of being self-employed is that you can often schedule your expenses and income to reduce your tax bill.

If you are a cash basis taxpayer, expenses you take before the end of the year (with a few exceptions) will reduce your tax bill. For example, if there is any equipment you need you should buy it before the end of the year. You don't necessarily have to put out a lot of cash — you can buy the equipment on an installment plan with a low down payment and still deduct the **full price** this year (up to the $10,000 limit) using the Section 179 Deduction.

If you are in the 15% income tax bracket this will save you 28.02% of the purchase price on your federal taxes alone (15% + 13.02% self-employment tax). Every $100 of expenses you take will reduce your tax bill by $28.

Basically what you are doing is reinvesting your money in your own business instead of paying it out in taxes. Of course if you have purchased the equipment on credit you will have to pay it off over the coming months, but if the equipment helps you make more money in your business, you are ahead of the game.

Another last minute way to reduce your taxable income (if you are a cash basis taxpayer) is to bill your customers a little later than usual in December. That way they will be paying you in January rather than right at the end of the year.

Tax planning is an ongoing process — You start by keeping good daily records so you know where you stand at all times — you can set aside the tax money you'll need, adjust your estimated payments or take steps to reduce your tax liability while you can. If you wait until April to start thinking about your taxes it is too late. Once December 31st rolls by you can't do much to help yourself tax-wise. The keys to staying on top of your tax situation are:

1. Keep good records.
2. Familiarize yourself with the basic tax laws that affect your business.
4. Take every legitimate deduction you are entitled to.
3. Monitor your tax situation regularly so you can plan ahead.
5. Get professional help and advice when needed.
6. Don't wait until the last minute.

GETTING MORE INFORMATION

The IRS publishes a number of free tax guides. Some of these guides have been mentioned in this chapter. You certainly don't need them all, but you should get a copy of Publication # 334, "Tax Guide for Small Business". Many public libraries carry current IRS publications.

The IRS has toll free numbers which you can dial to get free advice from tax experts on just about any tax problem. These numbers are listed in your phone book.

Chapter 15
RESOURCES

TRADE MAGAZINES

Building Services Contractor Magazine
MacNair Publications, Inc.
101 West 31st Street
New York, NY 10001
(212) 279-4456
Toll Free 1-800-622-6247

Cleaning Management Magazine
15550-D Rockfield Boulevard
Irvine, CA 92718
(714) 770-5008

Services Magazine
10201 Lee Highway, Suite 225
Fairfax, VA 22030
(703) 359-7090
Toll Free 1-800-368-3414

TRADE ASSOCIATIONS

Building Service Contractors Association International (BSCAI)
10201 Lee Highway, Suite 225
Fairfax, VA 22030
Toll Free 1-800-368-3414

International Sanitary Supply Association (ISSA)
7373 North Lincoln Avenue
Lincolnwood, IL 60646
(312) 286-2575
Toll Free 1-800-CAL-ISSA

COMPUTER SOFTWARE FOR BIDDING AND ESTIMATING

Cleaning Management Institute
15550-D Rockfield Boulevard.
Irvine, CA 92718
(714) 770-5008

CTS America
4501 Circle 75 Parkway, Suite F-6205
Atlanta, GA 30339
(404) 859-2535

Creative Management Systems, Inc.
400 Riverside Avenue, P.O. Box 41226
Jacksonville, FL 32303
(904) 355-2745
Toll Free 1-800-874-5554

Daniels Associates, Inc.
11240 North 19th Avenue, #23
Phoenix, AZ 85029
(602) 371-0152

Management Information Systems Corp.
35 North Montford Avenue
Baltimore, MD 21224
(301) 732-4437

START-UP INFORMATION

The **Small Business Administration** offers dozens of inexpensive pamphlets and books of interest to the contract cleaner. For example:

"Starting and Managing a Small Service Business"
"Business Plan for Small Service Firms"
"Handbook of Small Business Finance"
"Managing the Small Service Firm for Growth and Profit"
"Creative Selling: The Competitive Edge"
"Recruiting and Selecting Employees"
"Training and Developing Employees"

For a complete list of SBA publications write: SBA, P.O. Box 15434, Fort Worth, TX 76119. Request order forms SBA-115A and SBA-115B.

Small-Time Operator — How To Start Your Own Small Business, Keep Your Books, Pay Your Taxes, and Stay Out of Trouble!
A Guide and Workbook by Bernard Kamoroff, C.P.A.
Bell Springs Publishing
P.O. Box 640
Laytonville, CA 95454
(707) 984-6746

PROMOTIONAL MATERIALS

Full color sales brochures and presentation folders designed specifically for the janitorial contractor are available from:

Mollman Marketing
P.O. Box 307
Millstadt, IL 62260
(618) 476-1544

CARPET CLEANING INFORMATION

The Bane-Clene Professional Cleaning Digest
Bane-Clene Corp.
3940 North Keystone Avenue
Indianapolis, IN 46205
Toll Free 1-800-428-9512
Toll Free in Indiana 1-800-382-9899

Carpet Procurement & Maintenance For The Nineties
by Gordon S. Clausen
Clausen Marketing Associates
P.O. Box 76
Bryn Mawr, PA 19010

Installation & Cleaning Specialist Magazine
17835 Ventura Boulevard, Suite 312
Encino, CA 91316
(213) 873-1411

Taking the Mystique Out of Carpet Cleaning
by Brian Kepka
B.R.K. Enterprises, Inc.
336 South Donald Avenue
Arlington Heights, IL 60004

WINDOW CLEANING INFORMATION

American Window Cleaner (Trade Magazine)
27 Oak Creek Road
El Sobrante, CA 94803
(415) 222-7080

The Professional Window Cleaning Manual, How to Make Money In Your Own Window Cleaning Business
by Frederick R. Massey
MBM Books
P.O. Box 1087
Valley Center, CA 92082
(619) 749-2380

NATIONAL SUPPLIERS

These companies sell cleaning equipment and supplies through the mail. Write or call for their current catalogs.

Dura Wax Company, Inc.
1603 Palma Drive
Ventura, CA 93003
Toll Free 1-800-438-7292
Toll Free in Western States 1-800-338-3872

Hesco Inc.
6633 North Milwaukee Avenue
Niles, IL 60648
Inquiries (312) 647-6700
Toll Free 1-800-822-7467

Industrial Ladder and Supply Co., Inc.
1155 North Ellsworth Avenue
Villa Park, IL 60181
(312) 530-7580
Toll Free 1-800-833-0800

Jon-Don Products
451 Frontier Way
Bensenville, IL 60106
Toll Free 1-800-556-6366
Toll Free in Illinois 1-800-237-7738

Southwest Manufacturers, Inc.
3243 South Jones Street
Fort Worth, TX 76110-4397
Inquiries only (817) 926-8281
Toll Free 1-800-433-2913
Toll Free in Texas 1-800-772-2748

Carpet Cleaning Equipment & Supplies

Workmaster Professional Cleaning Products
P. O. Box 11518
Fresno, CA 93773
Toll Free 1-800-344-7224
Toll Free in California 1-800-742-1985

The Butler Corporation
251 Moody Street
Ludlow, MA 01056
Toll Free 1-800-535-5025
Toll Free in Massachusetts 1-800-458-4550

Window Cleaning Equipment & Supplies

J. Racenstein & Co., Inc.
Professional Window Cleaning Tools and Equipment
611-621 Broadway
New York, N.Y 10012
Toll Free 1-800-221-3748
In New York and Alaska (212) 477-3383
Toll Free from Canada 1-800-621-0056

L.M. Colker Co.
2618 Penn Ave
Pittsburgh, PA 15222
(412) 391-1955
Toll Free 1-800-533-6561

Uniforms & Work Clothing

TODD Work Apparel
P.O. Box 29107
St. Louis, MO 63126-0107
Toll Free 1-800-458-3402

OFFICE FORMS AND SUPPLIES

These companies sell business forms and office supplies through the mail. Write or call for their current catalogs:

The Drawing Board
P.O. Box 660429
Dallas, TX 75266-0429
Toll Free 1-800-527-9530

Grayarc
P.O. Box 2944
Hartford, CT 06104-2944
Toll Free 1-800-243-5250

New England Business Service, Inc. (NEBS)
500 Main Street
Groton, MA 01471
Toll Free 1-800-225-6380

INDEX

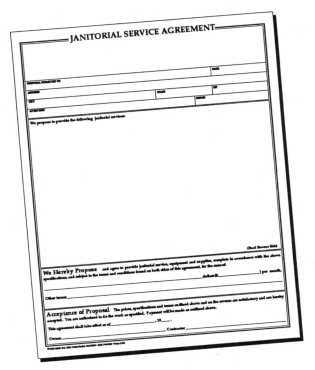

Designed for the Janitorial Contractor

BID FORMS

Quickly prepare a professional-looking bid using this one page form:

- Project a professional image and build customer confidence – win more jobs!

- Ideal for bidding small and medium-sized janitorial accounts.

- Contract terms and conditions spelled out in detail on the back.

- Shows potential customers you know your business.

Fill in at the job site for immediate customer approval and acceptance. For larger jobs attach a detailed specifications sheet. Type or stamp your company name in. 8½" x 11" size.

Pad of 50 forms only $9.95

THE PROFESSIONAL
WINDOW CLEANING MANUAL

by Frederick R. Massey

Learn how to make $15-$30 an hour in your own window cleaning business. Get the inside story on:

- How to estimate and bid, including sample bid forms and examples.

- Beginning and advanced techniques of window cleaning—fully illustrated.

- 20 ways to promote and expand your business.

- Equipment facts, how to get everything you need for as little as $50.

- Plus hundreds of useful tips and tricks of the trade...

SEND FOR YOUR COPY TODAY!
only **$14.95**

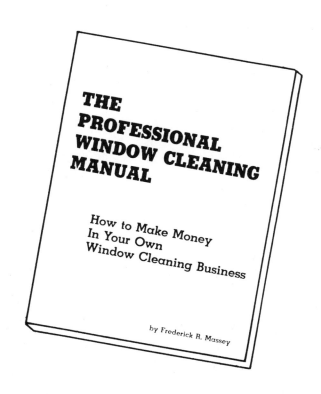

TO ORDER — Use the order forms on the following page, or call (619) 749-2380 and use your Visa, MasterCard or American Express credit card. ➡

Yes! Please rush me:

_____copies of *Inside the Janitorial Business*   @ $34.95 each $_____

_____copies of *The Professional Window Cleaning Manual*   @ $14.95 each $_____

_____pads of *Janitorial Service Agreements*   @ $ 9.95 each $_____

Shipping (Add $2.00 first item, 50¢ each additional item) $_____

California residents please add 7% sales tax $_____

TOTAL (U.S.Funds) $_____

SATISFACTION GUARANTEED!

❑ Payment enclosed (Make check or money order payable to MBM Books. No C.O.D.'s, please)

❑ Please charge my: ❑ Visa   ❑ MasterCard   ❑ American Express

Card number_____ Expiration Date_____

Signature_____ Daytime Phone (   )_____

Name (please print)_____

Company Name_____

Address_____

City_____ State_____ Zip_____

Send to: **MBM BOOKS, P.O. Box 1087, Valley Center, California 92082 USA** • (619) 749-2380

Yes! Please rush me:

_____copies of *Inside the Janitorial Business*   @ $34.95 each $_____

_____copies of *The Professional Window Cleaning Manual*   @ $14.95 each $_____

_____pads of *Janitorial Service Agreements*   @ $ 9.95 each $_____

Shipping (Add $2.00 first item, 50¢ each additional item) $_____

California residents please add 7% sales tax $_____

TOTAL (U.S.Funds) $_____

SATISFACTION GUARANTEED!

❑ Payment enclosed (Make check or money order payable to MBM Books. No C.O.D.'s, please)

❑ Please charge my: ❑ Visa   ❑ MasterCard   ❑ American Express

Card number_____ Expiration Date_____

Signature_____ Daytime Phone (   )_____

Name (please print)_____

Company Name_____

Address_____

City_____ State_____ Zip_____

Send to: **MBM BOOKS, P.O. Box 1087, Valley Center, California 92082 USA** • (619) 749-2380

Yes! Please rush me:

_____copies of *Inside the Janitorial Business*   @ $34.95 each $_____

_____copies of *The Professional Window Cleaning Manual*   @ $14.95 each $_____

_____pads of *Janitorial Service Agreements*   @ $ 9.95 each $_____

Shipping (Add $2.00 first item, 50¢ each additional item) $_____

California residents please add 7% sales tax $_____

TOTAL (U.S.Funds) $_____

SATISFACTION GUARANTEED!

❑ Payment enclosed (Make check or money order payable to MBM Books. No C.O.D.'s, please)

❑ Please charge my: ❑ Visa   ❑ MasterCard   ❑ American Express

Card number_____ Expiration Date_____

Signature_____ Daytime Phone (   )_____

Name (please print)_____

Company Name_____

Address_____

City_____ State_____ Zip_____

Send to: **MBM BOOKS, P.O. Box 1087, Valley Center, California 92082 USA** • (619) 749-2380